A BEGINNERS GUIDE TO

HUNTING
AND
TRAPPING
SECRETS

by
Dr. Duane R. Lund

Distributed by
Adventure Publications, Inc.
820 Cleveland St. S.
Cambridge, MN 55008

ISBN 13: 978-0-934860-52-9

A Beginner's Guide to
Hunting and Trapping Secrets

Copyright © 1988
by
Lund S&R Publications
Staples, Minnesota 56479

First Printing, 1988
Second Printing, 1990
Third Printing, 1996
Fourth Printing, 2002
Fifth Printing, 2007
Sixth Printing, 2010

799.2
LUN

10/12/10

Printed in the United States of America
by
Lund S&R Publications
Staples, Minnesota 56479

With special appreciation to the following consultants: Donald Hester, Cass Lake, Minnesota; Leo Jewett, Swatara, Minnesota; Jack Vantrease, Iliamna, Alaska

TABLE OF CONTENTS

Page

PART I HUNTING

PART II TRAPPING SECRETS

PART III WILD GAME RECIPES FOR KIDS

PART I
HUNTING SECRETS

INTRODUCTION
A GOOD HUNTER

- Puts safety first:

    - has gun loaded only when expecting to shoot momentarily.
    - makes sure the safety is on until the moment of shooting.
    - points the gun only at something he/she wants to shoot.
    - makes certain the correct gauge or caliber shell is being used; slightly smaller shells may lodge in the barrel causing a dangerous blow-out.
    - checks to make sure the barrel is clear of any obstruction at the start of each hunt. If the end of the barrel is pushed into the ground during the hunt, unload the gun and check to make certain it is clear.
    - carries the gun in such a position that if one should stumble or fall and the gun should go off no one would be injured.
    - observes common sense safety measures when hunting from a boat, including the wearing of a life jacket.
    - when hunting big game, wears the colors of clothing that state or province requires so that one is less likely to be mistaken for an animal or not be noticed in the line of fire.
    - only shoots when there is a good chance for a clean kill; does not shoot at birds or animals which are out of range; avoids wounding and losing game.
    - pursues wounded game, making every effort to make sure the bird or animal does not suffer and that the meat is not wasted.
    - takes good care of game so that the meat does not spoil. It is a special privilege to be able to enjoy eating wild game.
    - does not kill anything which will not be eaten.
    - when possible, hunts game birds with a trained dog which will find and retrieve birds. Not only will you have a better chance to shoot and find more game, but a dog adds greatly to the enjoyment of the hunt.
    - is courteous and considerate of other hunters; does not spoil shooting for them.
    - does not hunt on private land without asking permission.
    - observes all laws, including shooting hours and bag limits. Such laws are set for the purpose of giving everyone a chance to enjoy hunting now and for many generations to come. Because of good laws and good game management, some kinds of hunting are better today than ever. For example, there are more deer in the Upper Midwest today than in recorded history. There are more geese in the central and

Mississippi flyways than ever before. Also, new game birds have been introduced to our country, such as pheasant and Hungarian partridge. By observing sound conservation prac tices, hunting will continue to be an exciting and enjoyable sport. In countries where there have been no controls or planning, virtually all wild game has been eliminated.

CHAPTER I
DUCK HUNTING

Anyone who has not watched the sun come up over a set of decoys;

anyone who has not thrilled to seeing a flock of sixty or seventy bluebills settling in;

anyone who has not felt the heart pound a little faster as a flock of high-flying mallards responds to a call;

anyone who has not known the sting of wind-swept snow on a stormy day while rising out of the blind to take a crack at a pair of fast-moving goldeneyes as they cross the decoys;

anyone who has not unconsciously ducked as a pair of teal come in from behind and disappear out of range before you can even put a gun to the shoulder, almost knocking your hat off in the process;

anyone who has not admired a fully-colored drake wood duck;

anyone who has not watched with pride as a hunting dog returns from a particularly difficult retrieve and lays a plump bird in your hand;

anyone who has not known the enormous satisfaction of filling out early and then sitting back with a can of pop or a cup of coffee and a sandwich and enjoying October's exhilarating weather—watching ducks continue to decoy and then hurry away when you talk to them;

has really missed an important slice of life!

The challenge of successful duck hunting comes from learning all one can about the feeding and flight habits of these highly intelligent birds, and then, with the help of this knowledge, trying to out-think and deceive them. A second challenge is trying to hit them!

Here are some things to remember about all species of ducks:

- Ducks have excellent eyesight. If you can see them, chances are they can see you.
- High-flying ducks have a special advantage in seeing you or anything unnatural about your decoys or blind. Next time you are on a high hill or in a low-flying airplane, notice how much more you can see than when you are on the ground.

- Never look up at ducks flying over or circling; human faces are especially visible.
- Ducks are attracted to decoys by their color as well as their shape and formation. Remember this when painting or selecting decoys.
- Select camouflage clothing appropriate to the setting: greens for early fall and browns for late fall.
- Ducks are mostly concerned about moving objects. Even if you are caught in the open, remain perfectly motionless and the birds may still come in range.
- Ducks have excellent hearing; sneaking within range is difficult and hard work. If possible, work into the wind.
- Old market hunters say ducks have a keen sense of smell. Some experts do not all agree with this, but why take chances?
- Ducks rarely decoy or come into the same spot two days in a row, especially if there has been heavy shooting.
- Ducks are enormous eaters and will sometimes forget about danger if good food is available. This can be seen in city parks where even wild ducks throw caution to the wind and risk everything for a free handout of corn or bread. Learn where the food is and chances are you will find good hunting.
- Ducks trust other ducks and they like companionship—this is particularly true of the "divers", such as bluebills (scaup), ringbills, canvasbacks, and redheads. That is why decoys work well in attracting ducks within range. Of course, the birds probably also assume that the decoys are enjoying something to eat.
- Ducks are sociable. They talk to each other. This is why calling skills are so important to successful duck hunting.
- The feeding habits of ducks are somewhat like those of fish. There are certain times of day when they are more likely to feed. Ducks of all species have three primary feeding periods: early morning, midday, and evening. The noon period is not as good as the other two, except on dark or stormy days. Puddle ducks (such as mallards, teal, widgeon, wood ducks, and gadwalls) tend to feed at the "crack of dawn". Divers are a little later, with goldeneyes and ringbills coming first and bluebills (scaup) an hour or so behind. The

reverse is true in the evening; ringbills are the last to come in. Ducks in migration, however, may be "stocking up" for the long flight south or may be hungry from the flight in from the north. In this case they may eat anytime of the day or night. Nevertheless, mid-morning and mid-afternoon are usually the slow periods for duck hunting.

● Ducks do feed every day. Just because you don't see any where you are, don't assume there are none in the area. ***Move and keep moving until you find them.*** After all, the sport is called "hunting", not "sitting"!

Kevin Crocker, Big Lake, Minnesota, with a nice bunch of greenhead mallards.

- Ducks fly lower and move around more on cloudy, windy days. Some scientists believe they fly closer to the ground because of lower air pressure on most dark or stormy days. Perhaps the reason ducks move to sheltered areas on windy days is that they don't want to be tossed about on rough waves while feeding. Warm, still, sunny days are usually poor days for hunting ducks, except again, during peak periods of migration.
- Ducks migrate by the calendar as much as by the weather. Early or late freeze-ups may affect the migration, but the major movement of each species of birds will usually come within the same week or ten day period on the calendar. This is one reason keeping a diary of your hunting experiences is so important.
- Some ducks are smarter than others. Among the puddle ducks; mallards, blackducks, and pintails are thought to be the more intelligent. Teal and wood ducks are considered among the less wary. Of the diving ducks, greater scaup (the larger variety of bluebills), canvasbacks, ringbills, and goldeneyes are harder to deceive, while redheads and lesser scaup decoy more easily.

PUDDLE DUCKS

Puddle ducks are so called because they feed in relatively shallow water where they can reach food on the bottom without diving. Often only their tail feathers are visible as they stretch their necks under water to feed. Wild rice beds are a favorite habitat, but they also feed on wild celery, weed seeds, etc. Some puddle ducks (mallards in particular) may feed in grain fields.

Now we will take a look at each of the species of puddle ducks—or "tippers" as they are sometimes called—as found in the Upper Midwest and south-central Canada.

Mallards

Mallards have been called "the king of the ricebed"—the most desired of all ducks—beautiful to behold and excellent on the platter. The drake mallard is appropriately called a "greenhead"; however, during the summer months, like most ducks, they lose their colorful feathers and are difficult to distinguish from the hens. The tipoff—the drake's bill remains more green, and the hen's more orange. They are a large duck, up to 24 inches in length and three pounds in weight. Mallards breed throughout the world and are common to most parts of the United States and Canada. They also breed in the far north, and there is a remnant each year which do not move south until the ice deprives them of their feeding places. Most, however migrate through southern Canada in early October and the northern tier of states in mid-October, hitting the second tier of states (Illinois, Iowa, Kansas, Missouri, and Nebraska) in November.

The mallard is highly intelligent, and once shot at is difficult to decoy. They seem to respond best to a relatively small number of decoys (up to twelve). The author has carried only two or three decoys back into difficult places and had excellent shooting. Scatter the decoys in front of the blind—in range, but not too close. Avoid letting your decoys bunch together; this is a danger signal to incoming birds. It is interpretted by them as meaning an attack is expected. It is helpful to leave a large opening in the middle of the decoys for the mallards to target on as they approach.

Choose the location of your blind with great care. Pick a spot where you have seen birds feeding or where floating feathers indicate ducks have been there. It is best to be out of the wind, but it is ideal to be exposed to enough wind to give your decoys a swimming action. Ducks always approach decoys and land into the wind.

Greg Hayenga, St. Cloud, Minnesota, displays a mixed bag of Saskatchewan mallards, pintails, and geese.

Use as natural a blind as possible, making yourself completely invisible. Do not show yourself until the ducks are well within range and you are prepared to shoot. Mallards often circle a few times before coming in close enough to shoot. Have patience and keep your face down; do not move a muscle. Be sure there is nothing in your blind that will reflect the sun—such as a pop can or thermos cup. Wear clothing that blends into the surroundings.

Use your duck call to get the attention of a passing or high-flying flock. Once they see your decoys, change to a feeding call and talk them in. It is far better to call too little than to call too much. Tease the ducks in—don't overdo it.

Ducks on any given day will usually approach the decoys in the same pattern. Some days they are more cautious and will circle several times; on other days they will come in directly (especially opening day). Note the flight and approach pattern of the first flock; chances are others will come in the same way. When the birds are over your decoys with wings cupped and feet out-stretched, like landing gears on an airplane, it just doesn't get any better—let them have it!

Shoot crippled mallards as quickly as you can. Do not try to pick up crippled birds with your hands; they will dive and you probably won't see them again. They can swim long distance under water, or they may grab a weed with their bill and die in that position—not letting go.

If ducks do not show up, move!

Although decoy hunting is great sport, *jump shooting* is also fun as well as productive. A good time to jump shoot is mid-morning or mid-afternoon when decoy shooting is usually slow. Small sloughs and secluded bays are prime target areas. Mallards are very difficult to sneak on, so it helps if the day is windy. Stormy, dark days are the best. The crack of a twig may send them flying. Keep out of sight at all times. Move slowly. If more than one hunter is sneaking, take care to make certain the guns are pointed away from the hunters. Spread out before shooting. Agree ahead of time as to who will shoot to the left and who will shoot to the right when the birds flush. Try to work into the wind. Any hunter who can sneak within range of ducks has earned the right of surprise—the right to raise up, once within good range, and shoot as the birds take to the air. Puddle ducks, such as mallards, jump up a few feet before flying forward. Diving ducks take off across the water.

Another form of jump shooting is wading through thick water vegetation—not unlike hunting pheasants in a cornfield. Because of the vegetation, the ducks may not hear or see you until you are in range—particularly if you walk into the wind.

Pintails

Just about everything that has been said about mallards, also applies to hunting pintails. They will come into mallard decoys quite well, but if they are fairly common to the area you are hunting, a few pintail decoys off to one side will help. Because mallards and pintails often feed in the same ponds and may even be seen flying together, mixing the decoys will not frighten away either species.

Pintails are easily distinguished from other ducks in flight by their long necks and pointed tail feathers (especially the drakes). They are a little longer than mallards (up to 26 inches in length), but weigh less (about two pounds).

Wood ducks

These most beautiful of all ducks are a prime example of what good game laws and effective management can do for wildlife. Nearly extinct a generation ago, wood ducks are now among the most plentiful. Originally "woodies" nested in big, hollow trees. As the loggers took their toll, the birds had few places left in which to nest. Several years ago, it was discovered that wood ducks would nest in large, man-made bird houses. Soon many conservation groups, such as Ducks Unlimited, began constructing and erecting these houses across the United States and southern Canada. The rest is history. Woodies are a mid-size duck—about 19 inches in length and 1½ pounds in weight. Woodies will frequently come into mallard decoys and they enjoy much the same habitat. They are especially fond of acorns, however, and are frequently found in lakes, rivers, and streams where oak trees are plentiful. They usually begin feeding before sunrise; another prime feeding time is just before dusk. Beaver dams and small sloughs hidden back in heavy forests are excellent places to look for wood ducks.

Woodies may announce their coming with a unique whistle, rather than the quack associated with other puddle ducks. Once you have heard it, you will not forget it.

A crippled wood duck may swim away with just its bill above water.

Widgeon

Widgeon—also called "baldpate"—are another prize duck. The drake is an especially beautiful bird, with its large white patch on top of its head, green wing and eye patches, and chestnut brown breast. The meat is very tasty and lighter in color than that of most ducks. Widgeon enjoy the same habitat as mallards and are often seen feeding—or even flying—with them. They will not hesitate to come into mallard decoys. No special technique is required to hunt them. Like the woodie, it is a middle sized duck—smaller than the mallard, but considerably larger than teal (21 inches in length and 1¾ pounds in weight).

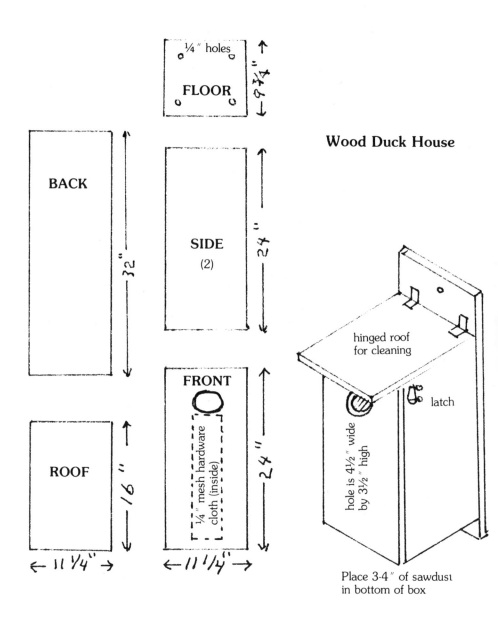

¼" holes

FLOOR

9¾"

Wood Duck House

BACK

SIDE
(2)

24"

32"

ROOF

16"

FRONT

¼" mesh hardware
cloth (inside)

24"

hinged roof
for cleaning

latch

hole is 4½" wide
by 3½" high

← 11¼" →

← 11¼" →

Place 3-4" of sawdust
in bottom of box

Suggested Design Plan For Wood Duck House

Eric Peterson of Lino Lakes, Minnesota, shows off ducks ready for plucking.

Gadwall

Although a middle-size duck (21 inches long and 2 pounds in weight), the gadwall hen is often confused with the larger mallard hen. It has essentially the same color and even quacks like a mallard (but softer). The drake, on the other hand, somewhat resembles the male pintail. It has a brownish head and gray, mottled breast. Both the drake and the hen have white wing patches, but the drake has a "splash" of brown above the patch. They are sometimes called "gray mallards" or "gray ducks".

Gadwalls are more common in western Minnesota, the Dakotas, and the Prairie provinces of Canada. They are often seen in sloughs along the highway. They are much less wary than the mallard and decoy easily. Although definitely edible, gadwalls are not considered to be quite as good eating as most other puddle ducks.

Bruce Lund, son Jack and Chad Longbella, all of Staples, Minnesota, with a morning's shoot of late season divers taken on Lake of the Woods.

Shovelers

Shovelers are also called "spoonbills" because of their over-size bill used in sifting through floating pond seeds and other slough foods. Although slightly larger, the shoveler is often confused with the blue-wing teal in flight because it also has a bright blue wing patch. It is a little larger than a teal, however—about 19 inches in length and 1½ pounds in weight. The drake is a beautiful bird with colors similar to the greenhead mallard, but the colors seldom develop until the bird has migrated south. The mating colors may be observed, however, when the birds return north in the spring. The spoonbill hen is easily confused with the hen mallard or gadwall, but is smaller and has a huge, flat bill. Not known as an intelligent duck, the spoonbill decoys easily and is not difficult to sneak on.

Bluewing teal

Although a small bird, (about 16 inches in length and one pound in weight), the bluewing is considered by many to be the finest eating duck. Unfortunately, they dislike cold weather and often head south after the first hard frost. This means most teal have left the northland by the time duck season usually opens. In fact, they leave so early, the drakes do not have their full color and are hard to distinguish from the hens. In the spring, however, the drakes are marked by a crescent next to the bill.

Teal decoy readily, even to mallard decoys, but they are a real challenge on the wing—a small erratic target. They appear to fly extremely fast, but are actually a little slower than the mallard.

Their quack is like that of an immature mallard.

Greenwing teal

The greenwing is the smallest of the puddle ducks (about 15 inches in length and less than one pound in weight). It is a hardier bird than its bluewing cousin and may be seen right up to freeze-up. The drake is a handsome bird with vivid green eye and wing patches and a chestnut breast. It is usually fatter than the bluewing and therefore a little more difficult to prepare for the table. It helps to parboil them first or at least drain off the fat when they are about half-baked.

Not only is the greenwing teal a very fast flyer (speeds approaching 70 miles an hour), but its quick, darting flight makes it a very difficult target. They often surprise the hunter by coming in low from behind or sneaking along the rushes just barely above the water. It is not unusual for them to show up in the decoys with the hunter wondering, "Now where did they come from?"

Cinnamon teal

Distinguished by its cinnamon-brown color, it is common in the West but rare in the Upper Midwest.

Eric Wolf, Sam White, and Kevin Kiffmeyer, all of St. Cloud, Minnesota, show off their mixed bag of puddle ducks and divers.

Black duck

The "black mallard", as it is often called, is a real trophy bird. Its dark feathers and contrasting red-orange feet make it a handsome duck, and it is the equal of its mallard cousin on the dinner plate. The black duck is fairly rare in the western upper Midwest and in the Prairie provinces, but it is quite common in Ontario, northeastern Minnesota, and Wisconsin. Known as a shy and intelligent bird, it does not decoy easily.

Black ducks are a little longer and narrower than the mallard (up to 25 inches long and 3 pounds in weight), and are easily distinguished by their dark plumage and royal blue wing band. The hen and drake have identical dark brown (not really black) feathers. Their feet are more red than those of a mallard.

Black ducks often decoy into "regular" mallard decoys.

DIVING DUCKS

Diving ducks are so called because of the way they feed. They have no difficulty picking snails or their favorite vegetation off the bottom of the lake in twenty feet or more of water. However, being a bit lazy, like all of God's creatures, they are usually found feeding in depths of from six to fifteen feet. Divers also differ from puddle ducks in the way in which they take off; they almost walk themselves off the water while puddle ducks take a small vertical jump off the water before flying forward. Diving ducks are also inclined to congregate in larger flocks than puddle ducks during migration. Flocks of resting birds up to several miles long have been seen on large lakes. They even fly and feed in flocks of more than a hundred birds.

"Sam", the black lab, checks out Bruce Lund's bills.

Generally speaking, diving ducks decoy more readily than puddle ducks—perhaps because they like to feed in large flocks. Their flight, however, is more erratic than that of the larger puddle ducks and they make a challenging target.

Diving ducks do not make a quacking sound. Bluebills (scaup) may be called by making a "Brrrrrrt" sound into a mallard call. If you let a single bluebill light in your decoys, it will probably talk to them. Try to imitate this sound. It is not as important, however, to know how to call scaup as it is to know how to call mallards.

When crippled, they will usually dive, but they will come up sooner or later.

Most diving ducks are not as brightly colored as puddle ducks.

Scaup

The greater and lesser scaups, known regionally as "bluebills", are the most common diving duck in this part of the continent. The greater scaup, sometimes called "northern bluebill", averages about a half-pound larger than the lesser variety. Greater scaup are about 18½ inches in length and 2½ pounds in weight. Lesser scaup are about 17 inches long and weigh about 2 pounds. The colors differ slightly in that the white feathers along the trailing edge of the wing run almost to the tip on the greater scaup.

The larger variety prefers bigger lakes and more open water.

Both the greater and the lesser scaup decoy well, and using decoys is the most effective way to hunt them. Larger "stools" of decoys are usually more productive; some successful hunters use as many as two hundred decoys. It is the author's feeling that fifty or sixty will do about as well as two hundred, unless you are competing with large rafts which are visible from your blind. If magnum decoys are used, the number may be considerably smaller—perhaps half as many. In fact, if the "bills" are around in large numbers and are decoying well, a couple of dozen decoys of any size is enough to help you limit-out.

The arrangement of the decoys is as important as the number. Almost any arrangement works well, provided you leave a pocket or opening in which they can land (if you were to let them). Ducks do not want to land in the flock.

The long string formation (out into the lake) is especially effective if the birds are flying by low over the water, and may have difficulty seeing your decoys. Another advantage of the "string of decoys" is that the individual decoys may be snapped onto a single line tied to your boat or to the shoreline; no anchors are needed. The decoys can, therefore, be put out and picked up more quickly.

Be sure you put out the decoys and position your blind so that your back will be to the wind. Ducks land into the wind. If the wind is blow-

Chad Longbella of Staples, Minnesota, Kevin Crocker of St. Michael, Minnesota, and Chris Longbella of St. Paul, Minnesota, show off the results of a day's hunt in Ontario.

ing into your blind the ducks will be forced to come in from behind you and will no doubt see you. Sometimes you will have no choice but to place your decoys in a cross-wind. This may cause the birds to light out from your decoys and then swim in, or your shooting may have to be as the ducks fly over your decoys as they cross in front of you. This makes a more difficult shot than if they are coming in with wings set.

If the wind is directly on your back, set the decoys a little to one side so that the ducks will not be looking directly into your blind as they settle in.

Although a good blind is always important, it is not as critical for diving ducks as for puddle ducks. If the migration is on and new birds are arriving daily which have not been shot at, it sometimes seems as though all that is necessary is to blend into the background and not move. Shooting will be better, however, if you are well concealed in a natural blind, made of materials found in that immediate area. Always wear appropriate clothing—especially the cap. Resist the temptation during slow periods to stand up or step out of the blind to look around. Remember that ducks have better eyesight than you do. Birds —especially bills—often seem to come out of nowhere and may not be seen until they are settling in.

As with puddle ducks, divers on any given day will have a set pattern of approaching your decoys. Watch for it. It will help you to be ready.

Points of land and small islands are usually good places from which to hunt scaup.

John Lelwica of Staples and Greg Hayenga of St. Cloud, Minnesota, with Lake of the Woods bluebills. No, they didn't shoot them all, just most of them!

If birds are flying past, just out of range, try calling them by sounding a "brrrrrrt" into your duck call.

If birds are not decoying but you can see them flying over another part of the lake, change your location. If you don't see any ducks, just don't assume they are not around. Get in your boat or car and look somewhere else.

Just because birds were at a given location one day does not mean they will be there the next day. If the shooting was heavy, they probably won't return. Duck hunting is rarely good in the same spot two days in a row. Even a slight change of location will help.

Try any of the following formations and see which works best for you:

Set #1

Two random groups with an
opening between them

Blind

Wind

Set #2

The "J" formation

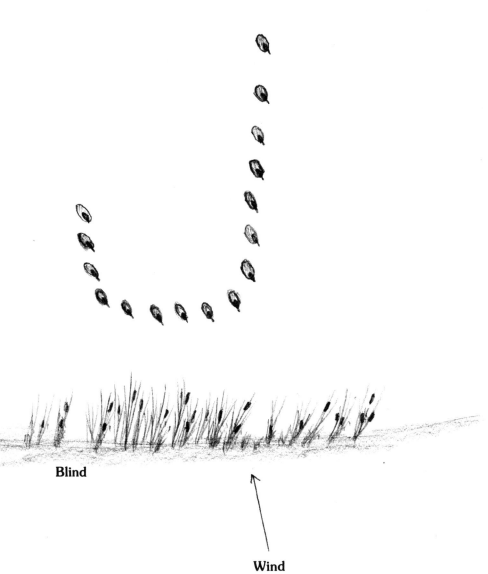

Blind

Wind

Set #3

The String formation

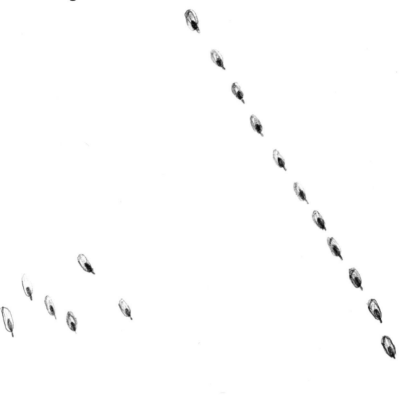

Blind

Wind

Ring bill (Ringneck)

Ring bills are more properly called "ringneck ducks", but because the ring which separates the head from the body is hard to see, the former name is the one most often used. Although the white ring on the bill is always there, it is more faint on the hen and is also less visible on the drakes in early season. The quickest way to identify a ringbill is to check the wing patch. Bluebills (scaup) have white wing patches; the wing patch of the ring bill is gray. Drakes in full color do have a distinct, ring-like separation between the head and the body. The head of the drake is basically black with purple and green iridescent hues—like the drake bluebill.

Ring bills are about the same size as the lesser scaup—about 17 inches long and 2 pounds in weight.

In contrast to bluebills, the ring bill likes bays and sloughs, including the edges of ricebeds. It does not like rough water and will seek out sheltered areas.

Ring bills are more cautious than bluebills and require greater care in selecting a blind. They will frequently circle several times before decoying. In fact, they may not decoy well at all and you may have to shoot on their nearest swing past the decoys. By watching each flock, you will soon know if that closest swing is on the first, second, or third pass.

Regular bluebill decoys work well for ringbills.

The favorite feeding time is early morning or late afternoon until dark. All too often they will come into a bay or ricebed after dark when you can't shoot. Ringbills often come in high, and on a quiet evening they will set their wings when they see your decoys and swing in like screaming jet airplanes!

Ringbills are **not** common to most parts of the country. The upper Midwest and southern Canada are their main habitat. Although they start their fall migration before the scaup, ring bills may be shot right up to freeze-up.

Many believe that ringbills, because of their wild rice diet, taste better than bluebills.

Canvasbacks

Just as the mallard is considered to be the "king of the ricebed", the canvasback may be called the "king of the open waters". It is indeed a prize duck. "Cans" were a favorite in fine restaurants at the start of this century and the market hunter all but wiped them out. Because canvasbacks follow a very precise route during migration and frequent a few special lakes on their way south, they have remained vulnerable to the sports hunter. In recent years, conservation departments have

A young lab's first retrieve.

*Three young St. Cloud hunters with Sam, the black lab, and a
mixed bag of Lake of the Woods ducks. Left to right, they are Sam
White, Scot Wolf and Greg Hayenga.*

designated many of these lakes as refuges. Hopefully, it will make a difference. It is interesting that their migration route brings them south, and then east across the Great Lakes to the Atlantic Ocean. The canvasback is the fastest of ducks, capable of flying over 70 miles per hour.

"Cans" will come into bluebill decoys. Years ago when the birds were more plentiful, hunters used over-sized "blocks" (as decoys are sometimes called) with red heads and gray backs. These decoys are now antiques and bring a special price on that market.

The drakes are especially handsome birds and hunters sometimes refer to them as "bulls". They measure about 22 inches in length and weigh up to 3 pounds.

"Cans" are a big water duck and frequent the same areas as the greater scaup. Occasionally, they will even fly together. Because of their size, heavier shot (#2 steel) is recommended.

Redhead

Canvasbacks and redheads are easily confused because they both have reddish heads. The redhead is smaller, however, and has a flatter, bluer bill. Also, the drake's head is more red than that of a canvasback. It has a gray wingpatch, which helps discern it from the female bluebill. Redheads are about 20 inches long and weigh around 2½ pounds.

Redheads prefer sloughs and bays to big, open water.

They are not a wary bird and, therefore, decoy quite easily to both mallard and bluebill decoys. Perhaps this explains their decline in numbers in recent years.

The redhead is another good-eating duck, and the drake is a beautiful trophy.

Goldeneye

Also called "whistlers" because their whistling wings may be heard great distances on a quiet day, the goldeneye comes in two varieties: the "Barrows goldeneye" and the "common goldeneye", which is slightly smaller. The Barrows goldeneye is about 20 inches long and weighs about 2¾ pounds. The common goldeneye is about an inch shorter and half-pound lighter.

The goldeneyes are a late season bird and among the last to go south.

They are fairly cautious and do not decoy well. Some authorities think this is more because they do not congregate in large flocks, rather than because they are particularly wary.

Bluebill decoys may be decorated with appropriate white markings and used effectively for goldeneyes. Just three or four of these specially painted decoys may be set to one side of the bluebill stool.

Dirk Manoukian of Reno, Nevada, with "Mandy", a black lab, and some handsome goldeneyes.

They are a tough bird to kill, partly because of their size and partly because of their heavy feathers in late season. #2 steel shot is recommended.

Goldeneyes have lighter colored meat than most ducks. The flavor, however, will vary depending on what they have been eating. End-of-season goldeneyes may be forced to feed on minnows and therefore taste a bit "fishy". Most of the time, however, they are excellent eating. Because of their size, they should be roasted a little longer than other ducks.

Goldeneyes seem to really enjoy rough water, and the bigger the lake the better.

Buffleheads

Buffleheads (or butterballs) look like small goldeneyes. The color pattern is different, but both birds have black and white markings. They have pink feet (whereas goldeneyes have yellow feet). The feathers on the heads of the drakes are usually "fluffed-up" making their heads look large for the size of their bodies; hence, the name—"bufflehead". Buffleheads are much smaller than the look-alike goldeneyes—about 14½ inches long and 1 pound in weight.

They are a good eating little duck.

Buffleheads often come into bluebill decoys. If you are interested in shooting more of them, paint three or four bluebill decoys with appropriate black and white markings and set them off to one side of the formation.

Although usually a big water duck, they will feed in sloughs and bays.

Eric Peterson of Lino Lakes, Minnesota, with a drake bufflehead.

Other Diving Ducks

Other divers which occasionally migrate through this part of the country include the big, black, white-wing scoter, the beautiful harlequin (an arctic duck), and the rudy duck—the smallest of all ducks on this part of the continent.

There are also several varieties of mergansers. They are distinguished from ducks by their long, pointed bills. Mergansers are not considered good eating.

PASS SHOOTING

Sometimes you may notice that ducks are consistently flying over a narrow strip of land between two lakes or past a particular point. You may have some real sporty shooting by positioning yourself there. Ducks usually fly much faster over a pass than over your decoys. You will find that you will have to lead them considerably farther—particularly if they have a tail wind.

Of course, hide yourself well.

WHICH GUN IS BEST FOR DUCKS?

The most commonly used shotguns come in a variety of sizes; they are (starting with the smallest) the 410, 20, 16, 12, and 10 gauge. At one time a 28 gauge was fairly popular but they are now quite rare and shells of that gauge are even more rare.

The 410 is a little small for ducks, unless you are a very good shot. Actually, the pellets will get out there and do the job. It's just that there are fewer of them in the pattern; thus, there is greater likelihood of missing or crippling a bird.

The 20 gauge and the 16 gauge both have enough shot to give a good pattern and have the advantage of being lighter than the larger guns and therefore quicker and easier to aim. The shells are also less expensive than for the larger guns.

The 12 gauge is the most popular shotgun, particularly for ducks. It has a larger and more dense pattern than the smaller gauges to help cover up your mistakes! If you are a young hunter, you may prefer to start hunting with a 20 gauge which is lighter and has less kick but still has good killing power. You may eventually choose to work up to a 12 gauge, or you may be so satisfied you will use it all of your life. Actually, a 3 inch, 20 gauge shell (requires a special barrel) is equivalant to a 2¾ inch 12 gauge shell.

The 10 gauge is really too big for ducks. It is unnecessarily heavy and awkward. It is even larger than necessary for geese, but may have a place for pass shooting at high flying birds. It has a tremendous kick and most hunters find they cannot shoot it very many times in any one day without getting a sore shoulder or a headache!

The next question is: what kind of gun—semi-automatic, pump, bolt action, side-by-side double barrel, over-under double, or single shot?

Bolt actions and single shots are usually cheaper and are good guns for beginners. They will probably give you only one good shot at a duck; this will teach you to take your time and to shoot well, making every shot count.

The automatic and the pump have the advantage of three shots. Some semi-automatics and pumps hold five shells; in such cases you are required to use a "plug" which limits the capacity to three (all you are allowed for migratory waterfowl). The automatic is a little quicker than the pump, but the pump is less likely to jam. Both, are excellent choices.

The double barrel (whether side-by-side or over-under) is quick, and you have the added advantage of each barrel featuring a different "choke". Choke refers to the control of the pattern of your shot:

full choke has the closest or tightest pattern. In other words, it covers the smallest area and has the greatest concentration of shot, and it is best for long range shooting;

improved cylinder has the most open or largest pattern with the least concentration of shot, and is best for quick, close shots; and

modified cylinder is in between. It is best for normal or "middle range" shooting. If your choice of gun allows only one choke, make it modified.

Years ago, most hunters used full choke. In recent years, most have moved to modified. This may be in part because there is less pass shooting today and more decoy shooting. Pellets from a modified or improved barrel travel just as far and hit just as hard as those from a full choke, but there are fewer of them in a circle of any given size at any given distance. Modified is ideal for most bird hunting, not just ducks. Improved cylinder is great for hunting upland birds, like partridges, in heavy cover, where you will only have a moment to aim and fire and where the birds usually flush fairly close. If you use a double barrel gun, choose one barrel modified and the other improved cylinder. Use the improved barrel first for close shots.

The polychoke is a device which may be affixed to the end of the gun barrel and adjusted for a variety of chokes. They are not as popular as they once were. You should also know that they tend to lower the resale value of an expensive gun.

"Multi-chokes" are available which screw into the end of the barrel of guns designed or tooled to receive them. Most hunters who have them seem to like them. It is cheaper than buying an extra barrel.

WHAT SIZE SHOT FOR DUCKS?

Duck hunters love to argue about size of shot, and each size has its defenders. Remember, the higher the shot number, the smaller the pellets and the more pellets there are in the shell. The lower the shot size number, the larger the size of the pellets and the fewer pellets there will be in the shell. Heavier shot has the advantage of greater penetration at long distances, but smaller pellets give you more room for error in aiming, simply because there are more of them in the shell.

In choosing shot size for ducks, you must keep in mind the kind of shooting you expect. You will need larger shot (possibly as large as size #2 steel) for long range shooting or in late fall when the ducks have heavier, thicker feathers. It is also true that the bigger ducks require larger shot, particularly at longer distances. In general, we recommend size #4 steel shot for early season and #2 steel shot for late season. If it is the end of the season and the birds are fully feathered, #2 steel shot may be the best—expecially for mallards, canvasbacks, greater scaup, or goldeneye. Anytime during the season when you find you are crippling a lot of birds, you may need to try heavier shot, or, you may need to aim better!

Generally speaking, lighter shot is better for decoy shooting and heavier shot for jump shooting or pass shooting. When shooting smaller or early season ducks over decoys, you can save money by using the cheaper low-base shells with less powder.

LEADING DUCKS

It is just not possible to tell someone how far to lead a flying bird. This will come with experience. The length of lead will vary according to how far away the bird is, how fast it is flying, and whether it is flying across in front of you, towards you, or quartering towards or away from you. In a way it is very much like playing basketball; by experience you learn good judgment and coordination. Some days, as with basketball, you will be hot and just not miss; othertimes you simply have a hard time hitting. Proper lead becomes even more difficult as we switch back and forth between hunting ducks or pheasants or partridges. Ducks simply move a whole lot faster.

Although we cannot tell you how far to lead a bird, we can tell you how to take that lead:

(1) hold on the duck
(2) move your barrel with the duck, keeping your site on it, and
(3) pull ahead of the bird, firing when you think you have the correct lead.

Actually, leading a bird is easier than it sounds. Practice will quickly pay off, and once you have the formula, it will come almost automatically. You will eventually take your lead and shoot by reflex, without taking a lot of time to think about it. This also has its hazards, however, and if you start missing, take a little more time to be sure you are selecting one bird and aiming. Don't pick a spot in the sky and then wait for the bird to get into the right position and then pull the trigger.

Don't let flocks confuse you; select a single bird and concentrate on it. "Flock-shooting" is just not productive.

Learn to swing your gun and to pull the trigger smoothly. Jerky actions are not helpful. A steady pull on the trigger will help avoid flinching and moving the barrel off target.

You can practice without shooting by following birds (any birds) with your gun again and again and again.

Trap shooting will also help your marksmanship. It may not be the real thing, but it is close to it and it definitely does help. It is especially helpful a week or two before the opening of season.

Most hunters miss because they do not take a long enough lead. If you miss on the first shot, try increasing the lead. Once you score it will be much easier to be consistent.

If birds are flying straight away, there is a tendency to shoot under them—because they actually are rising as they go away from you. If you are missing these shots, try raising the end of the gun barrel to cover the bird as you squeeze the trigger. The reverse is true if the birds are coming towards you with the intent of landing. Bottom line: there is no substitute for practice and experience.

CARE OF BIRDS

Ducks should be drawn (gutted) the same day they are shot. If it is a warm day, do so as soon as it is convenient and wash out the body cavity with cold water. Some people prefer to not pick ducks right away, especially during cool weather. Instead, they hang them by their necks for a few days to let bacteria action tenderize the meat. Not this hunter!

It is easier, of course, to remove the feathers before drawing the birds. Start by rough picking the ducks, leaving the down. Meanwhile, melt parafin wax in boiling water. (This should be done out of doors to reduce fire risk.) Remove one wing and the feet. Hold the duck by the head and the remaining wing and dip the rest of the bird into the water. It should come out well coated with wax. Let the duck cool until the wax is hard. Throwing it into the lake or a tub of cold water will hasten the hardening action. Scrape the hard wax off with a table knife. All of the feathers should come off with the wax.

If wax is not available, pick the birds as clean as you can and then burn off the down and remaining feathers by holding the duck over a flame. Again, do this outside. Another alternative is to dip the ducks (especially puddle ducks) in hot water to which enough detergent has been added to make suds. In our experience, the product called "Joy" works best.

Electrically driven duck pluckers also do an excellent job, and are not expensive.

Slit the rear of the bird with a knife and then cut both the windpipe and the esophagus in the neck. Pull out all of the entrails (guts), being especially careful to remove the lungs and voice box. If you hold the duck under water while doing this, the smell will be less of a problem.

Keep the birds in a cool place until cooking. Ducks may be frozen in freezer paper or foil, but if you plan to keep them for longer than a month, freeze them in water. Half-gallon milk containers work well.

DUCK HUNTING MEMORIES

There are so many good memories of duck hunts—from prairie potholes to wilderness ricebeds. Some were memorable because of bagged limits; some because of special fellowship; some because of the setting where the shoot took place; and others because of some special situation. This tale is a good memory because of a special holiday and a special dog.

The dog's name was "Jiggs". He was a relatively small, short-haired, short-tailed mixture of breeds. There was no way he should have been a hunting dog—but he learned to love the out-of-doors and even learned to tolerate cold water. I was nine years old when we acquired him. We had just lost the family hunting dog—a spaniel. It was Christmas time and my heart was broken. My parents realized the best way to heal the hurt was to purchase a quick replacement. My dad tried hard to locate a pup of any of the traditional hunting breeds—but none was to be found. I learned, however, that a neighborhood mut had given birth to a small litter of questionable heritage. When I paid a visit I fell in love with a little black pup with white markings. I begged and pleaded with my parents. My dad, as a hunter, knew better than to settle for a mongrel, but, after all—it was Christmas. I'm sure it was with great reluctance that he finally gave in and paid the two dollars the neighbors were asking.

As Jiggs grew, we tried hard to make a hunter of him, and after a couple of years we brought him to the point where he would chase down crippled ducks that fell on dry land. And he wasn't too bad at flushing pheasants and partridges, but he wouldn't retrieve any of them, he would just run over where they fell and stand there until one of us arrived. When this particular story took place, Jiggs was four years old.

It was the weekend before Thanksgiving, and we were allowed to hunt ducks quite late that year. It was one of those falls when the sloughs had frozen over, and then re-opened with the coming of "Indian summer". As we left the house before daybreak that morning, my mom suggested, "If you shoot some mallards we'll have them for Thanksgiving dinner."

My dad and I hunted potholes all that day without even seeing a duck. Apparently, most birds had paid more attention to the calendar than to the weather and had headed south. In the afternoon, shortly after we had enjoyed a lunch of hot venison sausages in home-made buns, the weather suddenly changed. Heavy clouds moved in on a brisk northwest wind and it began to snow—hard. There were still no birds, so my dad decided we had better head home before we had a problem with driving. The visions I had in my mind all day of mom's great Thanksgiving feast vanished. But a few miles from town, my dad suggested, "Let's make a quick check of Boomer's slough."

I was all for it. It was a small pond, surrounded by tall willows, just off the Mississippi River. It had provided many a good potshot in days past.

As we pulled within walking distance of the slough, the fury of the storm worsened. I remember pulling my coat collar up around my ears, and making my neck as short as possible to stay warm. We reached the water's edge and my father carefully worked his way through the thick willows until he could see open water. As he turned around to make his report, I knew from the look on his face there were no ducks—and that's just what he said, "No ducks."

Just then, out of the storm, three enormous mallards came in—wings set. My dad's 12 gauge automatic fired three times, slowly and deliberately as he took careful aim, and each time a mallard fell—dead!

Unfortunately, the birds fell too far out to reach them. The bottom of the slough was soft, and my dad's hip boots were of no help. We just looked at each other, hopelessly, and my father finally asked, "Now what?—If that dog could only retrieve."

Jiggs was always good about retrieving sticks or most anything else—except birds. I talked to him as though I expected him to understand every word and tried to explain how important Thanksgiving dinner was.

Seeing a stone at my feet, I picked it up and threw it in the direction of the ducks—something I had tried on previous trips but to no avail. But to our amazement, this time, Jiggs dashed into the water and swam to the nearest mallard. It was so huge he had to grab it by the neck—but he brought it in!

No dog ever received more praise—and he quickly retreived the other two.

Not only did we have our Thanksgiving dinner, but we had a hunting dog! In all his remaining ten years, he never let us down.

The author, as a boy, with "Jiggs", the mongrel who turned into a great hunting dog.

CHAPTER II
GOOSE HUNTING

If you like duck hunting, you will **love** goose hunting!

Maybe it's watching the huge flocks of geese fly south during migration—maybe it's their haunting call—maybe it's the huge size of the birds—whatever it is, hunting geese is a very special experience and any goose is a real trophy.

In the central part of the continent (the area we are dealing with in this book) the Canadian prairie provinces and the Dakotas have by far the best goose hunting. There are also a few excellent spots in Ontario, such as James Bay and Hudson's Bay. Minnesota seems to be getting a little better each year. There is also an excellent fall migration across Illinois, Nebraska and Missouri.

HUNTING OVER DECOYS

Most geese are shot over decoys, and the more decoys used, the better the chance of bringing in the birds. When there are heavy concentrations of geese around, small flocks of geese will respond to thirty or forty decoys, but usually it is well worth the effort to put out at least 100. You can get by with fewer decoys, however, if you are hunting on water.

Since setting out a large number of decoys is a lot of work, it is critical that you choose the right location. Most geese are hunted in picked grain fields. It is important to scout the area the day before to determine where the geese are feeding and to learn their flight patterns; although, if the wind shifts overnight, the birds may go an entirely different direction. Normally, the geese will come off the lakes where they spent the night shortly after day break. They will rise into the wind but then turn and leave the lake with the wind. They will spend most of the morning feeding in the fields and then return shortly before noon. They will again feed in the afternoon, but will probably not go so far from the lake. They will again return to water at dusk.

Most hunters use Canada goose decoys because this variety of goose is the most wary and because other varieties will often decoy into them. Of course, if there are mostly snow geese in the area, then white decoys would be more appropriate. Since each species of geese will feed with its own kind, it is a common practice to have a large set of Canada decoys and then set a couple of dozen white decoys off to one side (but in range).

Location of the blind

Where you build your blind is extremely important. Geese will detect anything unnatural from the air. Most field hunting is done from pits, and it is a good idea to cover up any fresh dirt with straw. It is also helpful to place the pit in among the decoys, using them to help disguise the blind. Sometimes the hunter can take advantage of natural cover, but geese usually shy away from fence rows or trees. Sometimes, one or two hunters can take advantage of a rock pile or a few small bushes as a hiding place.

If you are not certain a particular location is going to be good and you want to avoid digging a pit, try lying down among the decoys and covering up with camouflage netting. Usually you can find a spot with a little higher grain stubble or a patch of weeds. This does not work well with more than two hunters.

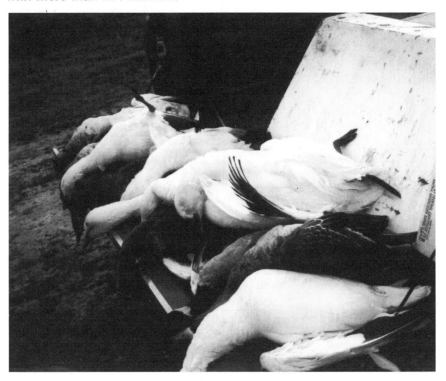

A morning's shoot of Texas snows and specs.

When hunting rivers, lakes, or sloughs, it is easier to build a good blind. Field decoys may be set in shallow water, on shore, or on sand bars. A few floating decoys will add to the effectiveness of the set.

In the prairie provinces or states, large lakes should not be hunted. If geese do not have a place to rest, they will soon leave the area.

Almost as important as the blind and the set of the decoys is the ability to call geese. This is not hard to learn. Calling is more effective if two or more hunters call at the same time. Good records and cassettes are available to help you learn the call of each species. The fact that some guides (particularly the Cree Indians) can call in geese **without decoys** and just by using their mouths (no call), shows how important it is to learn to call.

Geese, like ducks, will approach the decoys flying into the wind. It is very tempting for the inexperienced hunter to shoot too soon. The birds are so large they seem much closer than they actually are.

For most shooting over decoys, size #2 steel shot is large enough, however, BB size is also popular. Remember, lead shot is no longer legal for waterfowl in the United States.

Pass shooting

Because geese follow regular flight patterns on their way out to feed and on their return to water, it is possible for the hunter to get into a good position for productive pass shooting. Because the birds don't like to fly low over trees or other cover, a ditch makes an excellent hiding place. If geese are working the fields, one technique is to drive around until a large flock is found on the ground, feeding. Position yourself where geese joining or leaving the main flock will pass over you—but be far enough away from the flock so your shooting will not scare them up. As indicated earlier, pass shooting usually means high flying birds and heavy shot is usually desirable. When hunting in a country where lead shot is permitted, #2, BB, or 00 "buck" works well.

CHOOSING A GOOSE GUN

The 12 gauge is by far the most popular and really is large enough for more than 90% of the goose hunting. The 10 gauge may have a place for pass shooting, but the higher cost of shells and the punishment your shoulder will take make it hardly worthwhile. Is there an advantage to selecting a gun that shoots 3 inch shells? Yes. The longer shell has more powder and more shot and will therefore kill at a slightly longer range and will put more pellets in the air. The 3 inch shells burn a little more slowly; so, you must lead the bird a little farther.

Magnum loads are available for 2¾ inch shells and will usually do the job quite well. However, when you buy a gun, be sure it is designed to take the abuse of heavier loads. Many goose hunters load their own shells and have favorite formulas for greater impact and distance.

SPECIES OF GEESE

Canada Geese

"Honkers", as they are sometimes called, are easily identified by the large white patch on their cheek. Unlike most species of ducks, male and female geese have identical plumage.

Some biologists believe there may be as many as eleven sub-species of Canada geese, largely identified by size. The range is all the way from the small Hutchins goose, weighing six or seven pounds to the greater or magnum Canadas which may weigh more than twenty pounds. Canadas nest in the northern tier of states and all the way north to the arctic provinces. They begin their migration relatively early and most Canadian geese leave Canada by mid-October. There is always a remnant, however, which will move south just ahead of freeze-up.

As mentioned earlier, Canadas are the most wary species and are most effectively hunted with large numbers of decoys and well camouflaged blinds.

Tom Armstrong and Greg Hayenga, St. Cloud, Minnesota, with a mixed bag of Saskatchewan geese (specs, snows, and Canadas).

White Fronted or Specklebellied Geese

In their first year, both the male and female of this species have a white breast; older birds have dark specs, almost forming bars, across their breasts—hence the different names for the same species of goose. Because "specs" are a fairly large bird (averaging seven to nine pounds when mature) and because they are so good eating, they are a favorite of many hunters.

Specklebellies are not as shy as Canadas and usually decoy well. As they approach the decoys they may make a cackling sound and, therefore, are sometimes called "cacklers".

"Specs" are more common in the western Dakotas and in the prairie provinces. They are early migrators.

Snow Geese

These beautiful white birds with black wing tips are probably the least intelligent—or the least wary—of the geese. They will even decoy to white paper towels or napkins shaped to look like geese.

Snows are very hard to pluck without tearing the skin, so many hunters skin them. They are also considered less tasty than other geese. There are, however, a number of recipes which will make them delicious eating. (See the last chapter, Part I.)

Bruce Lund, Staples, Minnesota, with a greater snowgoose.

Immature snows are gray in color. The **blue goose** is a variety of snow goose and the two types will fly and feed together and interbreed. Blues are more common in the eastern part of the Midwest and prairie provinces.

It is generally believed that there are at least two varieties of white snow geese, the greater and the lesser. Smaller snows will weigh about five or six pounds, and the larger birds will weigh up to ten pounds. Snow geese are late migrators.

Ross's Goose

Once quite rare and protected, this smallest of North American geese is now on the increase. In appearance, it is almost identical to the snow goose, but it is only slightly larger than a mallard.

They are more common in the western prairie provinces and migrate early.

CARE OF BIRDS

As with ducks, clean your geese—or at least gut them out—the same day you shoot them. If it is a hot day, draw them immediately and wash out the body cavity with cold water.

Geese are surely the ultimate in bird hunting. Just seeing and hearing the flocks of migrating birds is almost reward enough for the hunter.

GOOSE HUNTING MEMORIES

What a magnificent bird the goose is! I still get as much of a thrill out of dropping a goose as shooting a deer.

One of my most memorable hunts took place in western Saskatchewan. It was in the Kindersley area, where in the fall of the year you can see or hear geese 'most anytime, night or day.

Three of us, Elmer, Doc and I, had already enjoyed three mornings of fairly good pit shooting, but we were still ten birds short of our limit and the next afternoon we were scheduled to head home. After lunch on that third day, we went out scouting for a place to set up the following morning. By the way, you can't hunt geese afternoons in that province; conservation authorities feel that by giving the birds a rest each day, they will be more likely to stay in the area. As we drove around, we saw several small flocks of Canadas lighting in grain field behind a small hill. A quick check revealed that the geese were lighting in and around a relatively small puddle in a low spot. There had been a lot of rain that fall and the geese seemed to especially like those wheat fields which had water standing in them. To our delight, there was a fairly large rock pile within range of the puddle—an ideal spot for a blind without digging a pit. We had learned the three previous days that the heavy Saskatchewan soil can be about as hard to dig in as a concrete highway!

We had little difficulty finding the home of the farmer who owned the land. When we knocked on the door to ask permission to hunt, a smiling housewife invited us in for coffee and homemade cookies, and quickly assured us we would be welcome to hunt their fields.

Unfortunately, overnight Elmer came down with a case of stomach flu and didn't feel anything like hunting the next morning, so it was up to Doc and me to get those last ten geese.

We were up long before dawn and arrived at the rock pile site while it was still dark. We had plenty of time to set out several dozen decoys in and around the puddle. Just as we put the last decoy in place, a big honker let out a loud squack just above our heads! It was the first of hundreds that would come in.

We nestled down behind the rockpile and covered ourselves with camouflage netting. Then the fun began as flock after flock—some less than a dozen and others over a hundred—appeared from over the hill and came gliding in towards the decoys—wings set and landing gears down! The action came so thick and fast it is difficult in retrospect to recall just what happened. My memory is a pleasant blur of seeing geese everywhere—milling overhead, approaching over the hill, and even settling into the decoys before we had a chance to shoot. I do recall one time when there must have been a couple hundred Canadas milling all around us—honking loudly. Doc and I didn't know where to shoot first. Finally Doc whispered, "Let's take 'em!" As so often happens when there is too much game to choose from, we shot badly and not a single bird fell! Nevertheless, in less than an hour we had our ten birds: eight Canadas and two Specs. It was over all too soon. But then we settled back to just watch the geese and enjoy hot cups of coffee from the thermos.

When we returned to the motel and hauled Elmer out of bed to see our trophies, he really had mixed emotions. He was glad we had limited out but sad to have missed all the action.

Profiles and Proportionate Sizes of Swans, Geese, and Puddle Ducks

Trumpeter Swan

Canada Goose

Snow Goose

White Fronted Goose
(specklebelly)

Pintail

Mallard

Black duck

Gadwall

Widgeon

Wood duck

Bluewing Teal

Profiles and Proportionate Sizes of Diving Ducks

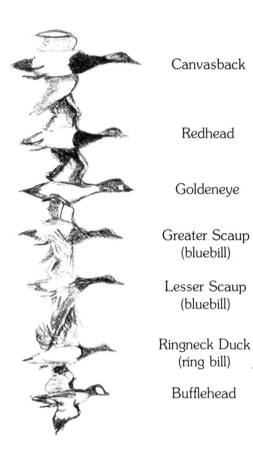

Canvasback

Redhead

Goldeneye

Greater Scaup
(bluebill)

Lesser Scaup
(bluebill)

Ringneck Duck
(ring bill)

Bufflehead

CHAPTER III
PHEASANT HUNTING

If the greenhead mallard is "king of the rice bed", and the Canvasback is "king of the open water", then surely the rooster pheasant is "king of the cornfield"! There are, indeed, few thrills in hunting greater than having a brightly colored, long-tailed pheasant explode from cover almost under your feet. Nor is there any fowl, domestic or wild, better to eat.

HABITAT

The secret to successful pheasant hunting is knowing where to find the birds. Unless you are prepared to do a great deal of walking with almost no action, it pays to travel to that part of a state which is best known for sizeable pheasant populations. Even when in that area, it is important to know what kinds of cover are likely to hold birds. Standing corn is usually excellent cover—if the land owner will let you hunt. (Farmers are concerned about hunters bending the stalks or breaking off ears.) Swamps, lakeshore cover, and the edges of sloughs near cornfields, soybeans or sorghum are excellent places to hunt. Idle farm land is another good place. Late season weather—especially when there is snow—drives pheasants into heavy cover, such as frozen cattail sloughs. Picked cornfields attract pheasants, but it is difficult to get in range. State and federal lands are usually open to pheasant hunting and are often planned and planted to attract pheasants. It sounds almost foolish to say it, but, "Hunt pheasants where they are!"

PHEASANT DOGS

A well trained hunting dog insures more flushes and fewer lost or crippled birds. Also, watching dogs locate and flush birds adds so much to the joy of a hunt. Setters and pointers are especially beautiful performers. Other varieties of dogs which are just as productive but which have a little less style, include labradors, spaniels, chesapeakes, and golden retrievers. Setters and pointers cover more ground but are often likely to range too far ahead; they demand that the hunter be in top physical condition. Unless a dog is trained to obey your command

The author, Kevin Crocker of Big Lake and Gordy Dezell of Staples, Minnesota, with South Dakota ringnecks.

and stay in close, it may do more harm than good. Obedience is the most important trait a good hunting dog can have. In conclusion, it is possible that a hunter will walk by more than 50% of the pheasants in a given area; a good dog will kick them up.

DRIVING AND POSTING

Driving is one of the most productive ways of hunting pheasants. Several hunters are needed to drive most areas effectively. The larger the area, the more hunters that are needed.

In addition to the drivers, a few hunters should "post" or stand at the end of the area to be driven. If it is a long drive, one or more hunters should stand on the side towards which the wind is blowing. As the drivers move along, the persons on the side should also move ahead. All hunters must be careful when they shoot. Pheasants often fly just above the corn or weeds. It helps if hunters have brightly colored caps and jackets.

Pheasants will usually leave the cover at the opposite end of where the drive starts or may fly out to the side—usually with the wind. Without posters, pheasants may just keep on running and never take to the air.

WEATHER AND PHEASANTS

Pheasants tend to hold better (and therefore let the hunter get in range) on windy, wet, stormy, or snowy days. When it is quiet, they are inclined to flush far ahead.

The nastier the weather, the more likely the birds are to seek cover. The worse the weather the heavier the cover they will seek.

GUNS AND SIZE OF SHOT FOR PHEASANTS

A rooster pheasant is a big tough bird—especially in late season. When working behind dogs and when experiencing close flushes, #7½ or #6 lead shot are good. For longer range shooting, it helps to have #5 or #4 shot. It is a good idea to have lighter pellets for your first shot and heavier pellets for your second or third shot.

A good formula to remember for the relative killing power of steel and lead shot is that steel needs to be two sizes larger. Thus, #4 lead = #2 steel.

The 12 gauge is the standard pheasant gun, but many hunters have success with smaller shotguns. The 20 gauge, for example, is easier to carry and quicker to point.

As stated earlier, if the barrel is designed to handle magnum three inch loads, the 20 gauge will be pretty much the equivalent of a 12 gauge with 2¾ inch shells and a standard load of powder and shot.

LEADING PHEASANTS

It is difficult to switch from ducks to pheasants and visa versa, because pheasants fly considerably slower (about 45 miles per hour). Because of their large size, however, they seem slower than they actually are. Practice will tell you where to hold. In a straight away or quartering shot, most hunters miss because they shoot under the pheasant. The end of the barrel should just about cover a rising bird.

Pheasants are not native to this continent and are an excellent example of how good game management can provide new hunting opportunities. Introduced to the Upper Midwest in the early 1900's, they were first hunted with real success in the 1930's. The dry years of that period made for more productive nesting and the birds had few natural enemies at first (such as the fox or skunk).

FIRST PHEASANT

Algonquin Indians had a marvelous custom of celebrating a young hunter's first successful hunt of each kind of game. They called it

"Ostenetahgawin", which means "feast of first fruits".

For most hunters, the first of a kind is remembered for a lifetime, and should be sufficient reason for a family celebration in this day.

My first pheasant is indeed a special memory—but I will never know for sure that I shot it!

My cousin, Dale, and I were enjoying our first hunting season with our own shotguns. Pheasant season had just opened—but we really didn't have pheasants on our mind that day. There just weren't that many around Brainerd, where we grew up. Actually, we had walked out the Duluth-bound railroad tracks to hunt partridges.

A couple of miles from town we left the tracks to follow Whitley's Creek to a favorite aspen grove. We were only a few steps into the tall grass along the tracks when this huge cock pheasant cackled his way out of the heavy cover. We both shot at exactly the same time, and the colorful bird folded and hit the ground with a thump—dead. Each of us, at exactly the same moment, uttered the words, "I got him!"

We stared at each other in disbelief and then asked simultaneously, "Did you shoot?"

We took turns fondling the beautiful trophy but then realized we both couldn't take the bird home—so we decided to draw straws. To make a long story short—I won.

We saw a few partridges that day, but Dale shot our only grouse. I really thought at the time he got him on the ground, but inasmuch as I had the pheasant, I didn't question him when he described his fantastic shot! Anyway, we each had a bird to bring home.

As we hit town and parted company, I took the longest way possible home. I strutted past every friend's house in that part of Brainerd—casually carrying the pheasant by its neck—the long tail sometimes touching the ground.

Both my parents were in the yard as I made my grand entrance—the timing was perfect. Even sharing the information with them that Dale and I had shot at exactly the same time did not detract from my triumphful homecoming.

I wonder if I would have told my folks the whole story if I hadn't been so sure Dale would have if I didn't?

My mom fixed a special dinner to celebrate my first pheasant. Of course, Dale was invited too!

DATE	TIME	SPECIES TAKEN	LOCATION	COVER	GUN	LOAD	DOG	WEATHER CONDITIONS	COMMENTS
9-15-88	7:30 am to 4:00 pm	4 mallards 2 teal 3 wood ducks	Rice Bay - Lake of the Woods Canada	lots of rice	1 auto 12 ga 1 over/under 1 auto 20 ga	#4 steel " "	Queenie	(N) wind ~ 15 mph, cloudy and cool	steady trickle of birds all day, not dumping v. well. Hunters: DRL, Chris, Kev.
10-19-88 and 10-20-88	7:30 to 4:00 both days	10 blue bills 3 ring bills 3 red heads	Brushy Tip Island Honeymoon Bay area	brush on shore in both locations	2 auto 12 ga 1 over/under	#2 steel "	Queenie	(N) wind - 20 mph - snow in the air @ times cool ~ cloudy	Cold !! Shot most of birds either early or late in day. Hunters: DRL, Candy and Jerry
11-3-88	10:30 am 4:30 pm	9 rooster pheasants	Brookings, SD, on Public Hunting areas	heavy; mostly cat tails and swamp	3 auto 12 ga 1 over/under	#4 steel	Queenie	light snow in air, 6" on ground	Shot nearly all birds in swamps near cut corn cover Hunters: DRL, Chad, Kev, Chris.

Keeping a hunting log will make you a more knowledgeable hunter.

CHAPTER IV
GROUSE AND OTHER
UPLAND GAME BIRDS

RUFFED GROUSE

Taking off from almost under your feet with thunder in its wings, the ruffed grouse, or partridge, has the element of surprise all on its side. By the time your heart drops from your throat back down to its normal position, the bird has usually darted behind the nearest tree or bush. On the ground, the partridge has another advantage: it is so well camouflaged that if it does not move, it is very difficult to pick out from its surroundings. An added problem is that the birds are usually found in heavy cover, and if the leaves are still on the trees, most hunters have to flush three or four birds for each shot.

Jack Lund of Staples, Minnesota, with his first two grouse.

Ruffed grouse are frequently found in aspen or birch groves and along the edge of swamps. They are also found in pine forests where they feed on berries—such as the wintergreen or high bush cranberry. They also like wild grapes and clover. In late fall or early winter when there is too much snow on the ground to find food, they will be seen in trees feeding on next year's buds.

Early and late season, partridges are found in coveys; when you jump one, watch for more. When flushed in thick cover, they will often light in trees, so when you follow a flushed bird, remember to walk very slowly so that you can look both high and low.

Explore the woodlands in the spring when partridges will betray their presence with the drumming of their wings. This is done to stake out their territory. Some biologists believe they also make this noise to attract birds of the opposite sex. Because partridges usually sit on a log when they drum their wings, many believe the noise comes from the wings hitting the log. Actually, this is not true. The sound is made by the cupped wings beating the air. The drumming sound starts slowly, and then speeds up toward the end—lasting only a matter of seconds. Because grouse stay in the same general area, you will find it worth while to return to any spot where you heard a lot of drumming in the spring. Partridges do drum occasionally in the fall.

Although partridges are tricky in flight, they are not hard to knock down—providing you can hit them! Light loads of powder with #7½ or #8 size lead shot is adequate. Either a 410 or 20 gauge is big enough, but the 12 gauge has the advantage of more pellets.

Good partridge dogs are hard to find. It is essential that they hunt in close because of the heavy cover in which birds are usually found. If you hunt without a dog, walk slowly, stopping to listen frequently for a "clucking" sound or birds walking in leaves.

The reward for the ruffed grouse hunter is one of the finest eating birds on the North American continent!

SHARPTAIL GROUSE

The sharptail or pinnated grouse is a prairie bird. It favors brushy, grassy areas where it feeds on insects, weed seeds, tender plant leaves, etc. In flight, the bird often makes a cackling sound, not unlike its arctic cousin, the ptarmagan.

Because they are usually found in open areas, they make an easier target than the partridge. They are also more apt to be found in coveys. When coveys are flushed, the birds will often scatter—much like quail. Then comes the challenge of locating them, one bird at at time.

Although not essential, it is very helpful to hunt sharptails with a good field dog. The birds will hold well for either a pointer or setter.

A nice mess of North Dakota sharptails.

Greg Hayenga, St. Cloud, Minnesota, with "Brandy" (his English Setter) and a handful of sharptails.

Because they often fly low, it is very important to make sure no other hunter, or even a dog, is in the line of fire.

The sharptail is a little larger than the ruffed grouse and the meat is considerably darker—but they are good eating.

SPRUCE HEN

The spruce hen looks a great deal like the partridge, except that it has darker feathers and a red spot under each eye. The meat is also darker, and is generally considered less tasty.

The spruce hen is found in the heavy forests of northern Minnesota, Michigan, and southern Ontario. They derive their name from the spruce swamps in which they are usually found. Spruce hens are considered to be one of the less intelligent game birds and will sometimes refuse to fly until their safety is seriously threatened. Some people claim to have killed them by using a stick as a club! It is no wonder they're sometimes called "fool's hens".

OTHER UPLAND GAME BIRDS

Woodcock

The woodcock (or timber-noodle) is one of the few upland game birds that migrate south for the winter. It begins its flight in September and is usually gone from the upper tier of states by early October. They may be found either in singles or in coveys, but if you jump one, you will probably find others in the immediate area.

The woodcock uses its long bill to dig worms and insects out of the ground and therefore may be found wherever there is soft soil, especially along streams and swamps. It likes the heavy forest areas and is often seen by partridge hunters. They fly with a quick, darting action, close to the ground and make a very difficult target.

Although smaller than the partridge, it has a large and tasty breast. Woodcocks may be easily confused with jacksnipes—which are quite a bit smaller and are usually found on lakeshores. They also have long beaks.

Jacksnipes are edible, but are not legal game in all states.

Hungarian Partridge

"Huns" were imported into the North cental states early in this century. Although they are a hardy bird, they have never been as plentiful as pheasants—with which they share the same habitat. In fact, they are usually considered to be a "bonus bird", picked up while hunting pheasants.

The Hungarian partridge is a small bird, only slightly larger than a quail. They are usually found in coveys but will scatter when flushed.

With a good bird dog, they may then be hunted out one by one. Huns are usually low flyers when flushed so the hunter has to be especially careful to be sure nothing is in the line of fire.

Light shot (7½ or 8 lead) is plenty heavy, but since you will probably flush them out of a cornfield or grassy cover while hunting pheasants, you'll likely be caught with heavier shot in your gun. Modified or improved cylinder choke would also be helpful.

The meat is darker than a pheasant, but tasty.

Quail

Found in the southern tier of Midwestern states, the quail offers some of the sportiest shooting of all upland game birds.

Its flight pattern is similar to the sharptail grouse or hungarian partridge and singles may be hunted once the covey has been flushed. A good field dog is essential. As a small bird, they can hide in light cover, thus giving the hunter full view of a dog's performance.

Quail are very good to eat, but not a whole lot bigger than a robin! The best quail hunting is found in the southern states.

Dove

Dove hunting is legal in only a few Midwestern states. Be sure it is legal in your state before shooting any. Doves are basically a field bird and are parital to agricultural areas. They are sporty on the wing and good eating. Although tricky in flight they are easy to knock down when hit. Use a modified or improved cylinder choke and #7½ or #8 lead shot with a light load of powder. The more pellets and the more open the choke the better.

Pass shooting is both fun and effective where there are fairly large concentrations of the birds. Pick a spot where they routinely fly going to and from their feeding or roosting areas. Of course, remain well-hidden.

Prairie Chicken

As the natural prairies have disappeared, so have these magnificent birds. Once very plentiful and seen in flocks numbering in the hundreds (and even in the thousands in our early history), they are now a rare sight in most Midwestern states; exceptions are Kansas and Nebraska where seasons are still held.

Prairie chickens are hunted much the same as their sharptail cousins. They are known for their spring mating dance and the "booming" sound they make with their orange, puffed-out cheeks.

GROUSE HUNTING MEMORIES

The first game bird I ever shot was a partridge. The previous Christmas I had received my first shotgun—a 20 gauge bolt action with a clip. I remember being so happy I slept with that gun the first night! It seemed like fall would never come—but it did. The first day of partridge season, my dad and I hunted some old logging roads that were so grown up with weeds and brush that vehicles no longer used them. There were a lot of partridges that year and by noon I had fired that new shotgun a dozen times, and that's exactly how many birds I miss-ed! My father was an excellent shot, and he made up for my inex-perience by shooting his limit and most of mine. Finally, he suggested, "I'm going to hold back; it's up to you to get the last two birds."

By then I was feeling pretty bad and had just about lost all faith in myself. But after a hearty lunch, my spirts rose and we hit the trail again. I can still show you the exact spot on that logging road—where it ran along a tamarack swamp—where we jumped the next bird. The dog was working an area off away from the swamp when a partridge exploded at my feet and headed for cover. The thunder of grouse wings still startles me, but I think it was worse then. Because of the bolt ac-tion, I only had time for one shot. I really aimed carefully, but when I shot, the bird continued untouched. Before I could feel sorry for myself, another partridge took off. I slammed the bolt home and took a snap shot just as it disappeared around a spruce tree. My dad yelled, "I think you got it!"

Just then a third grouse exploded out of a bush! I threw in my last shell and took a long shot at a fast disappearing bird. It started to climb—straight up—and then folded—falling like a rock—dead!

Without pausing to enjoy my success, I hurried to where I had last seen the previous partridge fly around the spruce. I found it before the dog did!

I kept my two birds separate from my dad's, and looked at them at least a dozen times on our way home. That night, when we cleaned the partridges, I cut off the tail fans of my two trophies and mounted them on the wall of my bedroom—where they remained until after my college days!

CHAPTER V
WHITETAIL DEER

FIRST DEER

As long as you live, you will remember your first deer. You will be able to recall exactly where you were, how you first saw the animal, what happened when you shot. You may even recall the kind of weather and the exact time of day.

I remember my first deer well. I was walking through heavy woods, shortly before dark on a beautiful November day. I had been "still hunting" on my stand and had given up hope of seeing an animal and decided to look around for a better spot for the next day. As I came upon an open area on a small hill, two deer suddenly came from my right and ran past me at about fifty yards. I fired four of the five shells in my 30-06 automatic and never touched a hair! It had been my first shot at deer and I was terribly disappointed. I turned to look back where they had come from, and there stood a third deer! I killed it dead in its tracks with my last shell. It was only a small doe, but that moment was one of the happiest in my life. A taxidermist friend made the four feet into an attractive gun rack, which I still use in my Lake of the Woods cabin.

I also recall my first buck especially well. I was walking in fairly open woods on a very quiet morning. Every step was noisy and I had little hope of seeing a deer, so I was hoping to find a good spot to sit awhile. Suddenly, I heard an animal crashing through brush and coming my way. Out of the thicket came an enormous buck, head down, running level to the ground, at about seventy yards. I fired all five shells as the deer passed but it never broke stride. He was soon out of sight in the heavy timber. I could hear him running a long while—and then a big crash. Fearing I had missed him completely, I hurried down to where the deer had run by me. My heart must have skipped a few beats with excitement as I discovered a wide blood trail! I followed it at a trot for about 200 yards—and then I saw him. The buck was lying in a small opening, dead; its magnificent head on a log looking at me. I counted the points from where I stood—ten long tines!

Back home, at the locker plant, the deer weighed 262 pounds—dressed out. It remains the biggest deer I have ever shot (or probably will shoot!). A handsome shoulder mount hangs on the wall of my bedroom.

Deer are highly intelligent and hunting them is a real challenge. They have every advantage—except, they don't carry a rifle (lucky for us hunters they don't!). Deer probably see as well as we do and their senses of hearing and smelling are far superior. What is more important, we are hunting them in their own back yard. They know every tree, rock, and hill.

Fortunately, deer do make mistakes. While avoiding other hunters, they may run or walk right to you. Sometimes, they may just grow careless. Or best of all, they may fall in love! Even a wiley old buck throws caution to the wind when he's on the trail of a doe.

Greg Hayenga, St. Cloud, Minnesota, with a fat Lake of the Woods "fork" buck.

BASIC TIPS

Here are some things to keep in mind while hunting deer:

- Hunt where the deer are. Scout the area in early fall. Look for deer sign (droppings, tracks, beds, bushes that have been chewed off, rubs on small trees where bucks have scraped velvet off their horns, and—as mating season approaches—ground scrapes).
- Get in the woods and stay in the woods. Not many deer are shot from roads or back in camp!
- Be where you want to stand before daylight—especially the first morning.
- When on stand, be very still and quiet. If you must move, move very slowly.
- When you walk, walk slowly and very quietly—stopping often to look and listen. Remember, hunters may see more deer while they are walking, but they shoot more deer when they are on a stand or sitting or standing still.
- Position yourself so that your body odors will drift into an area where the deer are least likely to come from.
- Be alert at all times. Depend more on seeing a deer than hearing it. If the woods are wet or if it is windy, it is very unlikely that you will hear it pass.
- If you are hunting with a scope in wet weather, keep it covered. Even a one inch section of a tire innertube works well. Of course, you can buy regular scope covers.
- Don't shoot until you are sure you have a deer in your sites you want to kill—especially in "bucks only" areas.

SELECTING AND BUILDING A DEER STAND
Looking for Sign

An experienced hunter can tell in a matter of minutes whether or not there are deer in the area. The animals leave tell-tale signs that are relatively easy to read, but you must be observant. Here are some key things to look for:

- Watch for droppings. Old, dried up droppings may

not mean anything. You may have just stumbled across last winter's deer yard. On the other hand, if the droppings are dark brown, soft and slippery—that's encouraging. Of course, the more you see, the more deer there probably are in the area. Also, the larger the droppings, the larger the deer.

Jack Lund of Staples, Minnesota, with his first deer.

- Look for "browse"—tender shoots of willow, aspen, or sumac that have been nipped off by feeding deer. Fresh cuts are most significant.
- Watch for "rubbings". Buck deer rub the summer velvet off their new antlers every fall. Look for small trees or heavy brush where the bark has been rubbed off from one to three feet above the ground.
- Look for "scrapes". During mating season, deer paw away the grass and leaves, exposing the bare earth; they then mark the spot with urine to let other deer know they are there. Deer will often make their scrapes under a tree where they can rub their brow glands against a branch. A moist mark on the branch means a deer was there a short time earlier. I have only seen bucks (never does) rub overhanging branches.
- Watch for deer trails. Although deer, when alarmed,may abandon traditional trails and travel in heavier cover, they will return to the trails as soon as they feel safe. Deer are like humans; they like easy walking.

Selecting a Site

Once you have located an area where deer sign encourages you to hunt, look for a site for a stand that will give you good visibility of at least one well-used trail. The edge of a swamp may also be a good site. Build your stand where the prevailing winds (usually west and northwest in the late fall) will blow your scent away from where the deer are likely to appear. Just getting off the ground will make it less likely the deer will smell you, but most states do have regulations about how high the platform may be. Of course, higher isn't always better. Choose the height that gives you the best visibility—but stay close enough to the ground so that an accidental fall is not likely to injure you.

Select natural materials for your stand. Look for a clump of trees or two or three trees standing close together. If there are only two trees close together where you want to build your stand, you may use a stout pole as the third support. Cedar is the best material; it is light and strong and will last several years.

Camouflage your stand from the platform up to hide your profile and movements. Spruce branches work well for this.

Cut out heavy cover that hinders your view of deer, but do not let the fallen trees or branches cover the trail. Carefully check from your stand to be sure you can see well. Of course, you don't want to cut out too much cover or the deer will not use the trail.

When you get in or out of your stand, **be sure to unload your rifle.**

Jack Lund's first trophy buck, taken at Leech Lake.

Make your stand as comfortable as you can, including a place to sit down. The more comfortable your stand, the more likely you will have the patience to sit in it until you see a deer. Some hunters even use small heaters on cold days. Remember, you want to stay in your stand just as long as you can; it really will pay off. Avoid making noise in your stand, and when you move, move very slowly.

Portable stands may be purchased or made, and they work—but, they are rarely comfortable. They do have one advantage, however, they may be easily moved if you don't see any deer.

It may be worthwhile having more than one stand. Use a stand in a more open area the first day of season, and then move to a stand in heavier cover starting the second day when shooting and human odors in the woods have made the deer more cautious and prompted them to move into heavier cover. This is especially true for bucks.

Deer sometimes rest a ways from where they feed. If you know where they are feeding and if you can locate deer beds, build your stand on a trail in between. The deer will usually move from feed to bedding areas in the early morning and will return towards evening. This does not mean deer don't eat during the daytime; they do not sleep all day, but will occasionally get up and browse close to their resting area.

Stay on your stand over the noon hour. Most hunters will head back to the car or cabin for lunch and may move deer into you.

Just because a deer stand is good one year does not guarantee it will be good the next. Check your hunting area a few weeks before season to be sure they are living there. Remember: hunt deer where they are!

DEER DRIVING STRATEGIES

As we have already said, most deer are shot by hunters on stands and the fewest deer are shot by hunters wandering around the woods by themselves. Hunting by the driving method is somewhere in between in effectiveness, but hunters who know what they are doing can be very successful—especially after opening day when deer are less likely to move unless they are pushed.

Huge areas of forest are hard to drive effectively. On the other hand, relatively small patches of woods or groves of trees may be easily driven—particularly if they are bordered by water, roads, or fields.

Here are a few rules for successful drives:

- Drivers should move with the wind so that the deer will smell them. Posters should stand where they are least likely to be smelled or seen.
- Posters should stand where they have a good view of deer leaving the sheltered area, as well as those which may turn back into the cover.
- Drivers should be close enough together so that the deer can not easily sneak back between them.
- Driving is the most dangerous way to hunt deer, so be very sure you do not shoot when another hunter may be in the line of fire.

ROTATING DRIVES

On the first day of season, stay on your stand all day if possible—from before dawn until as late as you can legally shoot. After that, a rotating drive may be an effective way to hunt and at the same time relieve boredom after the first couple of hours on the stand. Rotating drives work only among members of the same party, hunting in the same general area. Here's how it works. Simply take turns walking to each other's stand. Hunter #1 is chosen ahead of time to walk to the stand of hunter #2. Hunter #1 replaces #2 on that stand. Hunter #2 then walks to the stand of hunter #3, etc.—until the last hunter walks to stand #1, where he/she sits for about an hour and then begins the process all over again.

Walking hunters should move very slowly, stopping and sitting frequently. There is a good chance that he/she may shoot a deer while being still and an even better chance the driver will move a deer into one of the partners.

Chris Longbella, St. Paul, Minnesota, embraces a buck and a doe—just the right size for good eating.

HORN RATTLING

Does it work? You bet! But it may attract more hunters than deer!

Horn rattling is just what the words imply—rattling deer antlers against your stand and against each other. The purpose is to simulate two bucks fighting—just keep that in mind and create noise accordingly. After about twenty minutes, take a break of about equal length. Bucks are attracted by such fights and often intend to challenge the winner. Why do bucks fight? To chase other bucks out of the area so that the does in the vicinity will belong to them!

STALKING DEER

What are your chances of following deer tracks in the snow and getting a shot at that deer? Not very good—especially if the animal is a buck. Actually, you are better off sitting and waiting for another deer to come along. On the other hand, if other hunters from your party are on stand, it may very well pay to track the deer in hope of pushing it into someone else.

If you already have your deer, you can learn a good deal about animal behavior by following tracks. You will learn what kind of cover deer seek when alarmed, how they tend to circle behind you or position themselves to pick up your scent and keep track of you, etc.

Generally speaking, a hunter sees more deer by walking, but will have fewer opportunities to shoot a deer than on a stand or during a drive. But walking in the woods is a great experience and that's worth something!

If you must walk—

- Watch your step; don't make *any* noise.
- Take a few steps at a time; then stop and listen.
- Sit down frequently.
- Avoid tops of ridges or hills where your profile can be easily seen.
- Search out the woods with your eyes; you are more likely to see a deer than to hear one.
- Walk into the wind or into a cross-wind that will blow your scent away from the area where you expect to see deer.

SHOT PLACEMENT

This drawing shows the vital areas of a deer (or other big game). If the deer is very close, a neck shot is effective and will waste little meat. However, the safest place to aim is for the chest cavity, where the lungs, heart, and other vital organs are located. Although a deer shot in the chest cavity may not drop in its tracks, it will not run far.

A gut shot will usually, eventually, kill an animal—but a deer struck in the stomach or intestines can run a very long way. If you suspect your deer may be hit in that area, give it plenty of time—up to a full hour—to lie down and stiffen up.

TRACKING A WOUNDED DEER

Here are a few tips:

- If the animal "humps up" as you shoot, it is very likely hit.
- If the flag is down as the deer runs off, it may be hit. I have seen deer, however, run with their tails up even though mortally wounded.
- Wait at least a half hour before tracking the deer. Wait longer if you think the animal is gut shot or hit in a non-vital place.
- Check for blood. A deer may not bleed at first. Keep looking.
- Bright red blood means a lung shot. Dark blood indicates a muscle shot. Green fluid or forage means a gut shot.
- A dragging mark means a broken leg.
- Expect the deer to double back.
- If you jump the wounded deer but can't get a shot or miss, give it at least another half hour to lie down and stiffen up. Look for blood in its bed. The amount of blood will give you a clue as to how seriously it is hit.

BIG GAME RIFLES

The big game hunter has far more choices of rifles than anyone really needs. Yet each has certain special advantages. Some are designed for quick shots at whitetail deer in heavy cover at short range (such as the 30/30); some are designed for long-range shooting at antelope or mule deer in wide-open spaces (such as the .270 Winchester); others are designed for heavy clout with big game such as moose and bear—either close or at long distances (such as the .300 Winchester magnum).

The numbers indicated above indicate the caliber of the cartridge the rifle shoots. The name "Winchester", in this case means that is the name of the company that first developed the rifle that shoots that size cartridge. Other manufacturers may make the same size. The Remington Company, for example, may manufacture a .300 Winchester magnum.

Because there are so many different rifles available, we will not try to list them here. Excellent books are available which describe each in detail.

It should also be noted, that some cartridges are available in different bullet weights—always listed as grains. The heavier bullets will have more impact, but will drop faster when pushed by the same amount of powder. Thus, if you are hunting moose or deer at relatively short range with a .30/06, you may prefer a 180 grain bullet, but if you want to reach out for deer at longer ranges, you may prefer 150 grain. With a larger rifle, such as a .300 Weatherby you may choose 220 grain bullets for Kodiak bear or Alaskan moose (the world's largest), or may prefer 180 grains for longer range shooting at elk.

Few beginning hunters can afford to own several rifles, so you may ask, are there some that may be considered all-purpose? In my estimation, the .30/06 comes close. In recent years it has become the most popular rifle in North America. It is effective against anything from deer to elk or moose. Native Alaskans tell me that more Kodiak and grizzly bear are shot with a .30/06 than any other rifle. (Although this may be true, I would feel safer with a .300 magnum!) But the .30/06 does have enough hitting power for 'most any game and it can be sighted in for fairly long distances, but it does drop fairly rapidly over 200 yards. It also has a pretty hefty kick for young hunters.

The .30/30 has very little kick, but it is not very effective over 200 yards. Yet, if you hunt deer in fairly heavy cover, you will rarely get a shot over 75 yards and a .30/30 is all you need. Most native Saskatchewan moose guides I have known carry a .30/30 in the brush. Of course, they are not only very good shots, but they also know exactly where to aim.

If you plan to hunt both in heavy woods and in open areas—such as out West—then the 7mm (millimeter) is a good, all around rifle. It will bring down elk and moose as well as deer.

For my Alaskan hunting, I like my .300 Winchester magnum. It combines high impact power with fairly flat, long range trajectory (up to 300 yards).

In selecting a rifle, pay attention to the name of the manufacturer. Buying a "name brand" may cost a little more, but there is a better chance you will be buying a gun that will last you a lifetime.

Types of actions in rifles
There are four basic styles of rifle:
1. lever
2. bolt
3. pump
4. semi-automatic

Although each has its advantages and disadvantages, it will probably be wise to select the same action as your shotgun. It is very difficult to change over to bolt action when you hunt deer if you have been shooting ducks and pheasants all fall with an automatic or a pump. I know big game hunters who will argue that they want a bolt action because it is more dependable. As for me, because I hunt small game with an automatic, I would rather not have to think in a tight situation. I have tried hunting big game with a bolt action rifle, but all too often tried to squeeze off a second shot without throwing the bolt! But to each his own.

Generally speaking, pumps and semi-automatics are more expensive. There is also a tendency to shoot more cartridges and perhaps not aim quite as carefully, knowing you can fire another shot quickly.

On the other hand, many times I have missed a big game animal the first shot and had it stop because it was uncertain where the shot came from. With an automatic, the second shot has often been a sure thing. If I had to make the noise of throwing a bolt, the animal would be off running instantly, and I would have a much more difficult shot.

Rifle Sights

There are three common types of sights:

1. open
2. peep
3. scope

Without question, a scope is over-all the most helpful. There are times, however, when a simple open sight is more desirable—such as a running deer in heavy cover at close range. Scopes are available with tip-off mounts, so that you can use open sights in an emergency. The disadvantage of a tip-off mount as compared to a permanent mount is that they can be more easily knocked out of line by a bump or jar.

The peep sight is a good compromise, particularly for hunting on a stand.

The disadvantage of a scope is that it takes getting used to for fast shooting. This can be overcome with practice. Bring your rifle to your shoulder again and again until it comes up just right so that you can see through it clearly immediately and don't have to move your head back and forth. With practice, it will come up automatically, without thinking, first time—every time.

It is helpful to have a "variable scope", with different degrees of magnification (2 to 7 power, for example). Use the lowest power when walking, medium power on stand, and high power when hunting wide open spaces.

BOW HUNTING

Bow hunting for big game is a special challenge and it has its special rewards.

Because the bow is less effective at long distances than a rifle, the closer you are to a deer the better chance you have for a clean kill. Most deer killed by arrows are shot at under twenty-five yards. Because you have to wait for your target to come in range, you will probably see a lot more deer than when hunting with a rifle. It is also very likely that you will see several deer for each one that comes close enough to shoot at. So you will enjoy the suspense, each time wondering whether the deer you see will come close enough for a shot. This will add greatly, of course, to the excitement of the hunt.

To be in bow-range of a deer requires even more care and cunning than hunting with a rifle. If your state or province allows you to wear camouflage clothing, it is a good idea also to camouflage your face with grease paints (available in sports stores). Because the deer you shoot at will be relatively close, it is very important that you make no fast moves even though you are up in a stand. Whether you are turning your body or drawing your bow, do it ever so slowly.

Peter Odell, Staples, Minnesota, with his first deer taken with a bow.

Because you will probably find fewer hunters in the woods than during rifle season, and because nearly all bow hunters stay on their stands, there is little likelihood of another hunter pushing a deer to you. It is wise, therefore, to select a stand where deer will pass by on their way to feed (in the evening) and on their way to rest (in the morning). Usually deer are feeding before daybreak, but you may catch some late arrivals after daylight.

It really helps to spend some time in the field before season to learn the traveling and feeding habits of the deer in your area. If you plan to hunt in a farming region, it will be relatively easy to discover the fields in which they are feeding. Watch from a distance, probably with binoculars, to learn which trails deer are using as they come and go. Build your stand accordingly. It may be a good idea to have a couple of stands so as to allow for different wind directions. Clear out brush and small trees so that you will have an open shot, but do not change the cover so much that it will frighten the deer away. Eliminate nearby branches which you may not notice in the excitement of shooting and which could easily deflect your arrow if struck.

Although few hunters have an opportunity to shoot a deer while walking, it does happen. It is wise, therefore, to "notch an arrow" as you walk to and from your stand.

Good equipment is a good investment. A reputable sports shop will help you make good decisions in making your selections. A compound bow is a must. It is the single greatest advancement in archery since the long bow of the Middle Ages. Protect your arrow points and respect them. Although bow hunting has a far better safety record than rifle hunting, hunters have bled to death after falling on an arrow (usually as their stands collapsed or as they fell out of a tree). Arm guards and shooting gloves are also helpful.

Deer shot by arrow are frequently wounded. Review the tips for trailing a wounded deer as found in the rifle hunting section of this chapter.

Improve your accuracy by practicing before season. It is better to practice a little each day than occasionally for long periods of time. Practice will also help you get your arm and shoulder muscles in shape so that you can hold your pull without wavering while waiting for a deer to take that "one more step" into the open. Also, practice judging distances so that the sight on your bow will be more helpful. It is a good idea to pace off various distances from your stand so that you can make a quick, accurate judgment when a deer appears.

Cornfield Hunting

If stand-hunting bores you and you are tired of the frustrations of trying to get a decent shot while walking in the woods, try corn field hunting. It can be very productive. I have known several hunters who claim they get their deer nearly every year by this method.

Deer love standing corn, both as a source of food and as a place to hide or sleep. Frequently they may be found fairly close to the edges of the field. Success is based on walking very slowly along an edge of the field where the wind will blow your scent away from the deer. Stop at each row and actually peek around the end stalks, looking for deer.

They may be either standing or lying down. It is not unusual to catch one asleep. They can be surprisingly hard to see; look for an eye or an ear. If you see a deer in range, move very slowly back out of sight, draw your bow, and then just as slowly inch your way into a shooting position.

If the deer is out of range, estimate how much closer you need to be. Then slowly back up six rows. Walk up that row (ever so quietly) until you think you are in range. Then inch your way across the six rows. When you come to the last row, draw your bow and move into shooting position, one inch at a time. If the deer hasn't moved, he should be yours!

CHAPTER VI
SMALL GAME

GRAY SQUIRRELS

Squirrels are a great excuse to spend more time in the woods and to enjoy the great out-of-doors in the fall of the year. Frequently the season begins before and lasts longer than bird seasons or deer season. And gray squirrels are good to eat (not so with their red cousins!).

Successful squirrel hunting depends on two things:

    1. locating a grove of trees where they feed, and

    2. good marksmanship.

Gray squirrels are especially fond of acorns, so if you know of a grove of oak trees, that is a good place to start. The squirrel's food supply, however, is not limited to acorns; they also enjoy nuts, mushrooms, some fruit, and fungus (a mushroom-like growth on trees and rotted logs). Therefore, especially in years of short acorn supply, look in groves of other kinds of trees.

Marksmanship is important. Squirrels are not a very big target. Although the 22 rifle makes a good squirrel gun, you could use a shotgun if you so desired. Target shooting will help sharpen your eye. Every gun seems to shoot a little differently, so get to know your gun well; this is especially true of rifles.

One more bit of advice—try not to frighten a squirrel once you have seen it. Move slowly to get into good range. Make your first shot count. Once frightened, a squirrel is very good at hiding behind tree trunks or it may flatten out on top of a high limb where you can't see it. If this should happen, withdraw a little and just sit and wait. Squirrels are a curious animal and will eventually try to locate you.

RABBITS

It may surprise you to learn that more people hunt rabbits in North America than any other kind of game. So—don't miss out on the fun!

There are three kinds of rabbits in the Upper Midwest and the central Canadian provinces: jack rabbits, snowshoes, and cottontails.

The jack rabbit is the largest of the three and is usually found in farming areas. Look for them along the edges of fields, particularly in fence rows. "Jacks" are usually considered the least good eating, mostly because they tend to be a little tough. The flavor is excellent however, and if they are slow-baked they are quite good.

Snowshoe rabbits are somewhat smaller in size. They are unique in that they turn completely white in winter and are difficult to see against a snowy background. They are usually found in spruce or cedar swamps or along waterways.

The cottontail is the smallest of the three but is considered to be the best eating. It does not change color in winter, but is a light gray year-round. The cottontail may be found 'most anywhere in the woods—along rivers or streams, on high ground, among brush piles in cut-over areas, etc.

When there is snow on the ground, rabbit trails are easily visible. You might also look for piles of rabbit droppings.

Weather affects rabbit hunting. On dark days they will be on the move all day long; otherwise, they are most active in the morning and before dark. They usually seek shelter on stormy days.

Walk quietly; too much noise will drive them out too far ahead to be seen. If several are hunting together, make drives through likely cover, much as you would for pheasants—using drivers and posters.

Some people hesitate to hunt rabbits because of a disease called "tularemia." Although it is currently quite rare, it pays to wear rubber gloves while skinning rabbits; the disease can enter a human body through cuts. You can check for Tularemia by examining the liver. Infected rabbits have swollen livers with small white spots.

The 22 rifle makes a good rabbit gun, but rabbits are a tough target as they zig-zag through the brush. A 410 or a 20 gauge shotgun will shift the odds in your favor.

PART II
TRAPPING SECRETS

TRAPPING SECRETS
BASIC TIPS

Trapping has an exciting history. The need for new sources of furs to satisfy style-conscious Europeans was one of the reasons 18th century explorers worked their way west across the North American continent. It was also furs that brought trappers, traders, and voyageurs into the wilderness. Furs were the means by which Indians improved their standard of living as they traded skins for tools, firearms, cooking utensils, and warm clothing.

Today, trapping is not only an outdoor sport, but it remains financially rewarding as well. However, you should know "up-front" that trapping is hard work, will demand a great deal of your free time, and can even be dangerous. Nevertheless, when you approach one of your traps and see that it has been set off—and then pull a beautiful, trophy-size buck mink out of the water—you will quickly forget your cold hands and feet and the hours of walking. Suddenly, it's all worthwhile! Let's begin with some general advice:

- Safety first! Most trapping is around water. Beware of thin ice and deep holes. And don't get caught in your own trap!
- Dress properly.
  If you are working around water, hip boots or chest waders are a must—preferably insulated.
  In cold weather you will need gloves or mittens, and always bring a spare pair in case those get wet. Water-proof varieties are helpful when working with water sets, but you may need warmer gloves or mittens inbetween stops. Arm-length rubber trappers' gloves are essential when working water sets through the ice.
  Don't over-dress if you will be doing a lot of hiking.
- Keep traps clean and free of unnatural odors.
- Keep bait fresh.
- Have good equipment.
  The better traps tend to be more expensive, but they are usually more reliable and will eventually pay for themselves. Beginning trappers can often save a great deal of money by purchasing used traps from someone who has quit trapping.
  Carry a sharp axe or hatchet (with a guard).

If the ice is thick, carry a light-weight, sharp ice chisel (with a point guard).

Have a supply of flexible wire with you, and a pliers (which will also serve as a wire cutter.)

Use a knapsack to carry your equipment on your back—except for sharp equipment which could injure you if you fall. A small, plastic sled also works well.

- Use scent for dry sets (on land) to attract animals. Commercial scents may be purchased, but there are effective substitutes. For example, oil of anise works well.
- Don't set traps where they are visible from the air or you may catch owls and hawks. Most areas have laws prohibiting such open sets.
- For centuries, trappers have made their own scent from the castor glands of beaver. Each beaver has two of them—near the tail. Dry them until they are hard, then shave off little pieces with your knife whenever you need scent to attract furbearers to your traps. Scent also serves to cover-up human odors.
- Take good care of your furs; this will increase their value. Wash them with mild, soapy water. Dish washing detergent works well.
- It is very difficult to learn how to skin an animal just by reading about it. Since skinning is so important to the value of your furs, we suggest you ask an experienced trapper to show you how. Also, you will find it helpful to practice on squirrels and rabbits. Many present-day fur buyers would rather you didn't skin the animals yourself. Check with your buyer before season for his preference. If he would rather you did not skin the animals, I suggest that you:

  Clean the fur with mild, soapy water.
  Let it dry.
  Place each animal in a plastic bag.
  Freeze. Once frozen, keep animals frozen. Do not let them thaw and re-freeze.

- Be a humane trapper. Do not let the animals suffer. When possible, set your traps so that the animals will quickly drown. Use rocks, scrap iron, or other weights attached to the chain. Quick drowning will keep the animal from struggling free or chewing off its leg.

Tend your traps regularly and often. Check every day if possible.* Not only will this keep animals caught on land sets from suffering needlessly, but it will keep predators from chewing on the carcass. Even mice can damage your trophy.

- Mark your sets in such a way that they will be easy to find—even after a snowstorm. You may want to make a written record, along with a map.
- Be a good sportsman. Do not infringe on someone else's trapping area.
- Be a conservationist. Don't completely trap out an area (or a beaver house for example). Save some to reproduce for next year.
- For dry sets, before season leave some bait near where you plan to trap so the animal will come to look for food and even expect it without being afraid.
- Practice setting your traps at home before season.
- When setting your traps, bend the jaws toward the trigger so that they will lie flat.
- Check trapping regulations for your state or province so that you do not break the law. When in doubt, call the local warden.
- If you cannot remove a hide from a board, put it in the freezer for an hour or two and it should come off more easily.
- In most areas, a size 220 Conibear is the largest you may use on dry land (so a dog cannot get its head in-to it).
- Do not use wire stretches on racoons, fox, or mink -use boards instead.
- Do not over stretch a fur; the hide will appear to have a thinner pelt.
- Be sure to get the bone out of all tails with fur on them.
- Laws in most areas require that each trap be tagged with your name and address.

*Some state laws require checking land sets daily.

BEAVER

Beaver live in lodges or in dens in the soft banks of rivers or streams. In either case, they will betray their presence by freshly cut brances and tree limbs. Do not bother with lodges or dens that do not have freshly cut (green) wood—freshly chewed.

Tips for beaver sets:

- Choose a site some distance from the lodge or den. Some states have regulations as to how close you may trap. If you are too close, you will catch the young beaver (kits); these have little value and are really your future trapping. The older, larger beaver do their cutting farther from the house—often 100 yards or more. Look for areas where beaver are working.
- Cut a stout pole long enough so that when you push the one end into the mud (hard), the tip will be about one foot out of the water. If the pole is not pushed firmly into the bottom, the trapped beaver will pull it away.
  If there is ice, cut a hole about one foot across.
- Wire a bundle of popple or willow twigs just under the water (or ice) as bait.
- Fasten the trap just below the food. It should also be fastened by its chain to the bottom of the pole, so that the trapped beaver cannot surface and breathe. The object is to drown the animal as quickly as possible.
  You should weight the chain with a rock or scrap iron so that when the trap comes loose from the pole, it will keep the beaver from surfacing. Usually about a four-pound weight will do the trick. Of course, the end of the chain must always be fastened to the bottom end of the pole.
  Some trappers knotch the pole (like the barb on a fish hook) so that the ring at the end of the chain can slide down the pole but will be caught on a knotch if the beaver tries to swim up.
  You may choose to cut a heavy enough pole so that a small platform may be built below the food to hold the trap—so that everything lies flat. With a steel trap bend the jaws towards the trigger.

- Use a large enough trap (check regulations). The Conibear (330) is expensive but most effective. Otherwise, a double spring #3 steel trap is ok. A #14 Victor or a #44 Blake will surely do the job if your laws permit traps that large. A #4 Newhouse is also a good beaver trap.
- Check your traps every few days, particularly if there is ice—so it won't get too thick to chisel easily.
- If you happen to catch the mother beaver, the buck will leave. It is the female's house and if you catch a buck, she will stay there and another buck will move in. Young beaver usually move out after the first year.

A baited, shallow water set works especially well just before freeze-up, providing it is located on the edge of a drop-off so that there will be enough water to drown a trapped animal. Stick a number of popple or willow twigs in the shallow water—as if they were growing there. Set one or two traps between the twigs and the deep water. Secure the traps to a stout pole; be sure the chain is long enough to permit the beaver to dive into the deep water. Attach about four pounds of scrap iron or rock to the chain to drown the animal.

Dried castor gland chips or other scent in addition to the twigs may be placed on the shore.

Where legal, traps may also be set in beaver dam spillways. (Use a Conibear trap.)

Skinning Beaver

As we have already said, it is difficult to learn how to skin an animal just by reading about it—or even from drawings. It is better to find a trapper who will let you watch. It is also likely that your fur buyer will prefer a whole animal. In that case you must either bring it in right away or freeze the animal. Because beaver are so large, there isn't room for many in a typical freezer, but if the weather is cold, you may hang them outside. (Don't let them thaw and re-freeze.)

Here are some suggestions for skinning beaver:

1. Begin by cutting off all four paws and the tail. A hatchet or large clipper works well. Leave the arms and legs as part of the fur.
2. Using a sharp knife, cut the belly of the beaver open, starting at the tail and going straight up to the teeth, splitting the lower lip.
3. Remove the hide with a sharp knife—pulling as you cut.

4. Stretch the hide on a large piece of plywood fur side
   down. Begin by nailing (small nails) the nose to the board
   (towards the bottom). Take hold of either side of the hide
   at mid-point, and tack it to the board. Now tack the opposite side. Then, tack the end of the hide opposite the
   nose—towards the top of the board. Now tack the hide at
   four additional points, each midway between the four nails
   you already have in place, stretching as you go. Again,
   tack the hide at points half-way between the nails you
   already have in. Continue until the hide forms a circle (or
   an oval) with the nails less than 2 inches apart.
   Lastly, nail the paw holes closed.
   Many trappers draw different size circles on plywood, then
   choose the circle which best fits the size of each beaver.
5. Using a draw-knife (or regular knife), scrape off the excess
   fat. Let the pelt dry before removing it from the board.

OTTER

Otter are usually found on rivers or streams or lakes which have
streams running through them. You can locate otter by looking for
slides on banks (into the water). Also, watch for clam shells (a favorite
food of the otter). Otter seem to like to be around beaver—or where
beaver have been.

Tips for otter sets:
- Make your sets near slides or feeding areas as
  described above.
- The best lure we know of is beaver castor gland
  shavings. Save the two castor glands found near the
  tail of the beaver. Let them dry until they are quite
  hard. Using a knife, cut chips or shavings and place
  them on the shore near your set. Otter love to roll in
  castor chips. If you cannot get castor glands, use
  pieces of fish, preferrably smoked fish. We know one
  veteran trapper, who says fish works better as bait if
  you chew the fish a few seconds and then spit the
  pieces out by your set.
- Choose a spot where there is a drop-off into deep
  water by the shore. Set the trap in the shallow water.
  Chain the trap to a stiff pole; pushed hard and deep
  into the bottom. Attach about a four pound weight to
  the chain so that the otter will drown when it heads
  for deep water.

Tips for skinning otter:

- Otter are difficult to skin, so sell them whole if you can. Remember to clean the fur first with mildly soapy water. Freeze individually in plastic bags.
- To skin an otter, start by cutting a pole about 6 " in diameter.
- Gradually tape about eighteen inches of the smaller end of the pole, bringing the last six inches to a point. Sand the entire tapered surface smooth.
- The object is to turn the otter inside-out with the point sticking in its nose.
- Start by cutting down the back legs (beginning at the ankles) to the hole. Cut the hide around the paws. Split the tail until you can strip over the tailbone.
- Pull inside-out, over the tip of the pole.
- Much fat will stick to the skin. Remove this with a dull drawing knife.
- Let dry before removing the pole. (Freezing speeds up the drying process).
- A poor skinning job will decrease the value of any fur.
- If you have trouble getting the hide off the pole, freeze it for an hour or two.

MUSKRAT

Muskrat are among the easier animals to trap. Their hides are usually not as valuable as other animals, but you can make up for that in the numbers trapped.

It is easier to trap muskrat just before freeze-up; it saves chopping through frozen houses or through the ice (where either is legal).

Tips for trapping muskrat:

- Set a trap (#1½ jump or larger) on either side of a rat house on the flat spots they use for resting places.
- Chain the traps into a long stake pushed into the mud. More and more trappers are using the Conibear type of trap. They are clearly better in shallow water where a trapped rat cannot drown.
- When trapping after freeze-up, chop into the house, set the trap, chain it, then cover the hole over.

(Check trapping regulations in your state or province for legality.)

- Where legal, traps set in runways used by the muskrats are effective.
- Floating two or more traps on a board in open water is also a good technique. Cut or drill a large hole in each end of the board. You can then anchor the board by driving a stake through each hole into the mud. If the water level changes, the board can then ride up or down on the stakes.
- Muskrats and other furbearers (such as mink and otter) often use small creeks for travel and may be trapped by placing a small log across the creek at water level. Chop out a section the size of your trap. All of the log, except the chunk you chopped out, should be above the water. As the animal swims through the opening, it will step into your trap, set on the section of log just under the water.

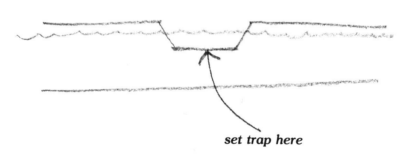

set trap here

Tips for skinning:

Muskrat hides are stretched (inside-out) on half-inch, tapered boards or on wire stretches.* It is the same process as used for otter, except boards are used instead of poles. Muskrats are much easier to skin than otter. Cut off the tail of the muskrat; it has no value. Freeze dry the fur for a few days, then remove from the board.

*Many trappers believe a board results in a better hide than a wire stretcher.

MINK

Because mink like to eat fish, crawfish, and other water creatures, these animals will usually be found along the shores of lakes and streams. Water-filled ditches are also a good bet.

Tips for trapping mink:

- Build a little house of natural materials (sticks and bark) up against the base of a tree, near water on the edge of a lake or stream. Make the roof out of bark or dead branches. Use sticks to narrow the doorway to the house and to guide the mink into the trap. The house as two purposes: (1) to guide the mink into the trap, and (2) to hide the bait and dead mink from owls, hawks, etc.
- Use both bait and scent. For bait, use pieces of fish, preferrably smoked, (smoked, because it doesn't spoil as fast and because it gives off more odor) or pieces of raw chicken—the bloodier, the better. For scent, use oil of anise or beaver castor gland shavings, or urine from a mink you trapped earlier. You may also purchase mink scent. Sardines work well too.
- Wrap the bait in screen so mice and shrews will not eat it up.
- Fasten the bait and the trap to the tree. Build the house over both.
- Set the trap between the bait and the door of the house so that the mink will have to step on it to reach the bait. Lay a limb or other object in front of the trap so that a mink will have to jump over it and into the trap as it tries to reach the bait.
- Use a #3 trap. Pull the pan down so that it has a "hair trigger".
- Sprinkle a little fine, dead grass over the trap to camouflage it—but not so much as to hide it completely. Dip the grass in scent.
- Check your traps daily so that mice or shrews will not ruin the hide.
- An easier and often more productive technique is to wade into streams or water-filled ditches and scoop out a pocket in the bank at water level. Place bait in back of the pocket out of the water and the trap in

front of the bait just under the water. Wire the trap
to a bush or anchor it in some other way. A Conibear trap in front of the hole works well.

Use the same procedure for skinning as with a muskrat—except use a
longer and narrower board. Let dry before removing.

WEASEL

Use the same techniques as for mink; however, weasel may be found
anywhere in the woods, not just near water. They are especially fond of
woodpiles or brush piles or may be found in or near meadows.

Use a smaller "house" and trap than for mink. A cardboard box with
a hole cut in one end works well. Place the bait inside the "house" and
set the trap on top of the bait (just below the hole).

For bait, use chicken parts (the bloodier the better).

Skin the same as a mink or muskrat (turn inside out), but use a
smaller board and leave the tail on.

MARTEN

Marten are found in remote, wilderness areas and are quite rare, except for certain parts of Alaska and Canada. There are two basic
techniques for trapping marten:

1. The house method as described for mink. Since the
   marten is twice the size of mink, use a larger house and a
   larger trap.
   The same bait and scent work well.
2. Lean a pole (about ten foot long) against a tree. Secure
   the bait to the pole. Tack the trap in place on the pole
   below the bait. Chain the trap securely to the pole.

FISHER

The fisher is similar in appearance and habits to the mink, but it is
considerably larger. Although sometimes found near water, it is more
apt to hunt inland. Look for them in mature timber. Its food is not
limited to water creatures, but includes rabbits, squirrels, mice, etc.

Use the same trapping techniques as for mink, but use a larger house
and trap.

FOX

The fox has well-earned such descriptions as "sly" and "cunning". It is
particularly wary of human odors—especially the older animals. Look
for fox in more open areas, including farm land. They feed on mice,
rabbits, immature birds that cannot fly, or 'most anything they are able
to catch.

Tips for trapping fox:
- Use the carcass of a skinned animal as bait.
- Sprinkle scent around the set. Use a commercial variety or urine from a fox you have taken earlier.
- Small pieces of fish (preferrably smoked) may be spread around the set (even if you also use a carcass as bait).
- Use two or three traps per set.
- Anchor the traps to a heavy limb or log.
- Cover the traps with thin tissue paper or light snow.

The hide need not be stretched.

RACCOON

Look for trails and footprints along shorelines of lakes, streams, and sloughs. Watch for paths through canebrake. Raccoons love corn, and may be trapped in the rows. Because raccoons are creatures of habit and follow their regular trails or paths, you need not use bait or scent. Camouflage the traps lightly with grass; anchor them well to a large limb, log, or tree. If none of these are available; use a stake.

Live traps, baited with fish guts or table scraps, are very effective. The raccoon is often more curious than wary. Hides need not be stretched. Skin them out as you would a squirrel or rabbit.

Check laws for trapping on dry land (such as size of trap). Do not place traps where they are visible to owls or hawks flying overhead. Do not trap where pets may be in the area.

PART III

WILD GAME RECIPES FOR KIDS

WILD GAME RECIPES FOR KIDS

Roast Duck

Wash each bird thoroughly inside and out, being careful to remove every trace of lungs, windpipe, etc.

Season with salt and pepper, inside and out.

Stuff with quarters of apples or onions—or 'most any vegetable you have handy, including potatoes or carrots.

Place birds in roaster or baking dish, breast sides up. Place one or two strips of cheap, fat bacon on each breast.

Add one cup of water (more if you are preparing several birds in a large roaster). Or—use ½ cup water and ½ cup cooking wine.

Cover, and bake in medium oven (300°) for 2 hours or until you can wiggle the drumsticks.

Goose Fillets With Onion Soup Mix

Cut the breasts from the carcass of a goose. Remove the meat from the legs and thighs (with a knife).

Lay the boneless goose meat on a sheet of aluminum foil. Put a large pat of butter on each breast fillet and another pat on the trimmings from the legs and thighs.

Pour the contents of one envelope of dry onion soup mix over everything.

Fold the aluminum foil over the meat and seal by rolling the edges of the foil together.

Bake in a medium oven (300°) for one hour and fifteen minutes.

Check to see if it is done; if not, return to the oven until tender.

Pheasant in Sour Cream

> 2 pheasants, cut into sections
> 1 small onion, diced
> 2 stalks celery, diced (½ cup)
> 2 cups sour cream
> ½ cup flour
> 2 T salt
> ½ T pepper
> ⅓ cup cooking oil

Dissect the birds including cutting the breasts of each bird into four pieces. Separate the legs from the thighs. Mix seasoning into flour and roll each piece therein. Brown slowly in frying pan in oil. Remove pheasant pieces and cook onion and celery pieces in oil until soft (about 5 minutes over medium heat).

Place pheasant in casserole dish. Mix onion and celery into sour cream and pour mixture over meat. Cover and bake in 325° oven for 1½ to 2 hours or until tender.

Wild Rice and Partridge Casserole

    1 cup wild rice (washed)
    flour
    1 partridge—deboned and cut up into pieces
    1 large onion, chopped
    1 green pepper, chopped
    1 small jar pimentos
    1 can mushroom soup
    1 can water
    salt and pepper

Basic Recipe For Preparing Wild Rice

    3 cups of water
    1 cup of wild rice (washed)—makes 3 cups cooked rice
    salt and pepper
    ¼ lb. melted butter or margarine

Season water with one tablespoon salt and bring to a boil. Add rice and lower the heat so that the water just simmers. Cook—covered—for about 45 minutes or until the kernels are well opened and the rice is tender. Do not overcook.

While the rice is cooking, cut the bird into bite-size pieces, removing all bones. Season, roll in flour and fry in oil slowly over low heat until browned but not "crusty". When it is done, add the chopped onion, green pepper, and celery. Continue frying for another three or four minutes. Add pimento, soup, and water.

Place all ingredients in a greased casserole. Cover and bake in a 300° oven for 1½ hours. Add water while baking to prevent dryness if necessary.

Tenderized Venison Steak (Cube Steak)

Round steak is often tougher than other cuts and is a good candidate for this treatment.

Sprinkle a generous portion of flour over each steak and vigorously pound it into the meat. Ideally, you should use a mallet designed for the job; however, the butt end of a table knife will do the trick. Turn the steaks over and repeat.

Now fry the steaks on a hot griddle or in a hot pan lightly coated with oil. They will get done quickly—about four or five minutes to the side if they are about a half inch thick.

Or, you could use a barbeque grill.

Baked Venison Steak

2 pounds steak (trim away fat)
1 26 oz. can (large) tomato soup
1 can tomato sauce
1 can water
1 cup chopped celery
1 large sliced onion
1 small, sliced green pepper
salt and pepper

Season steaks and arrange in single layer in baking dish or pan.
Add chopped celery, sliced onion, and sliced green pepper.

Cover with soup mixture (tomato soup and equal amount of water
and tomato sauce). Be sure meat is covered by liquid. If you prefer a
spicier sauce, add catsup or a couple of drops of Tabasco sauce. Place
in preheated 300° oven for two hours.

Jack Rabbit Mushroom Casserole

1 large jack rabbit
2 cans mushroom soup
1 oz. can mushroom stems and pieces

Soak the rabbit in salt water overnight. Dissect into pieces. Dredge in
seasoned flour and brown over low heat. Place pieces in a greased
casserole. Cover with mushroom soup, adding enough water to completely cover all pieces of meat. Add the mushroom stems and pieces.
Bake in a 325° oven (covered) for 1½ hours or until tender.

Baked Squirrel

4 squirrels, dressed* but left whole
2 large onions, quartered
1 large onion, sliced
4 slices bacon—the fatter the better
salt and pepper inside and out

Place in baking dish, side by side, back sides up on top of the
quartered onions. In other words, stuff the body cavities with onion as
best you can. Cut bacon slices in two and place on backs of squirrels
alternately with onion slices. Cover and bake in 350° oven between
1½ and 2 hours or until tender.

*dressed means skinned, head and feet cut off, and guts taken out.

A SPECIAL RECIPE FOR THE TRAPPER

Roast Beaver

1 young beaver (10# or under)
4 onions, 2 whole and 2 sliced
1 cup red cooking wine
½ cup vinegar
6 strips bacon

Dress animal*; remove all fat. Add vinegar to 2 cups water and wash beaver thoroughly. Soak 2 days in salt water solution (in cold place). Pat dry. Place in roaster. Cut two whole onions in half and place in body cavity. Slice other 2 onions and lay on beaver—alternating with strips of bacon. Place cooking wine plus ½ cup water in bottom of roaster. Cover and bake for about 20 minutes for each pound of animal or until very tender so that the meat can be easily removed from the bone. Strip all meat from the carcass and serve on a warm platter.

*dressed means skinned, head and feet cut off, and guts taken out.

A rewarding two weeks of trapping red fox by Bob Wonders and his son, Doug, in the Staples area.

Other Books by Duane R. Lund

A Kid's Guidebook to Fishing Secrets
Fishing and Hunting Stories from The Lake of the Woods
Andrew, Youngest Lumberjack
The Youngest Voyageur
White Indian Boy
Gull Lake, Yesterday and Today
Lake of the Woods, Yesterday and Today, Vol. 1
Lake of the Woods, Earliest Accounts, Vol. 2
Lake of the Woods (The Last 50 Years and the Next)
Leech Lake, Yesterday and Today
The North Shore of Lake Superior, Yesterday and Today
Our Historic Boundary Waters
Our Historic Upper Mississippi
Tales of Four Lakes and a River
The Indian Wars
Chief Flatmouth
101 Favorite Freshwater Fish Recipes
101 Favorite Wild Rice Recipes
101 Favorite Mushroom Recipes
150 Ways to Enjoy Potatoes
Early Native American Recipes and Remedies
Camp Cooking, Made Easy and Fun
The Scandinavian Cookbook
Cooking Minnesotan, yoo-betcha!
more than 50 Ways to enjoy Lefse
Entertainment Helpers, Quick and Easy
Gourmet Freshwater Fish Recipes
Nature's Bounty for Your Table
Sauces, Seasonings and Marinades for Fish and Wild Game
The Soup Cookbook
Traditional Holiday Ethnic Recipes - collected all over the world
The Life And Times of THREE POWERFUL OJIBWA CHIEFS,
Curly Head Hole-In-The-Day the elder, Hole-In-The-Day the younger
Hasty But Tasty
Fruit & Nut Recipes
Europeans In North America *Before Columbus*
Hunting and Fishing in Alaska
German Home Cooking
Italian Home Cooking

About the Author

- EDUCATOR (RETIRED, SUPERINTENDENT OF SCHOOLS, STAPLES, MINNESOTA)
- HISTORIAN (PAST MEMBER OF EXECUTIVE BOARD, MINNESOTA HISTORICAL SOCIETY); Past Member of BWCA and National Wilderness Trails Advisory Committees;
- SENIOR CONSULTANT to the Blandin Foundation
- WILDLIFE ARTIST, OUTDOORSMAN.